Sex Matters:
Men Winning the Battle!

Freedom that Lasts

D1502702

Waylon O. Ward

Copyright © 2004 Waylon O. Ward
All Rights Reserved

Printed in the United States of America
ISBN: 0-9761313-0-7
Library of Congress Number: 20-04096625

All scripture quotations, unless otherwise indicated, are taken from
the HOLY BIBLE, NEW INTERNATIONAL VERSION®.
NIV®. Copyright © 1973, 1978, 1984 by International Bible Society. Used by permission of Zondervan. All rights reserved.

Reproduction in any manner, in whole or in part, in English or any
other language, including usage of electronic, mechanical, information storage or retrieval systems, or any systems developed in the
future, without the express written permission from the publisher
and author, except by a reviewer, under the Fair Usage Doctrine, is
strictly prohibited. Any unauthorized use of any of the contents of
this book may result in civil penalty or criminal prosecution. This
copyright is registered with the U.S. Copyright Office, Washington,
D.C., and is protected under copyright law, and internationally with
all member countries of U.S./foreign copyright treaties.

Dedication

This book is dedicated to

Maurice E. Wagner

He has been my counselor, mentor and friend for 40 years. In writing this book, God reminded me of the many ways He has used Maurice to shape my counseling, my speaking, and my life. I am most grateful to you, Maurice, for allowing God to work through you.

God is not unjust; he will not forget your work
and the love you have shown him
as you have helped his people and continue to help them.
Hebrews 6:10

Acknowledgements

This book is a gift God has enabled me to write. I give Him all the honor and glory. He allowed many people to contribute to this project and I am grateful to you all.

- Thank you to the men and women who honored me by allowing me to counsel with them over the years. You will never know all that I learned through your stories and our interaction. But without you this book would not have been written. It was a privilege to share in your lives.

- Thank you to the men and women who have mentored and counseled me over the years. I am a better man because of your willingness to participate in and encourage me on my journey.

- Thank you to the twenty or so readers who took the time to read the working copy of this manuscript and gave us their input and feedback. I am most grateful to you for your assistance.

- Thank you to all the writers who touched my life over the years through their books and articles. Please keep writing. There are those of us who need your input.

- And last and most significantly, thank you to my wife, Lynn. It would take a book to detail my gratitude to you for your unconditional love and acceptance, belief in me, partnership with me as wife, lover and fellow writer. Your tireless efforts in editing and typing this manuscript made this book possible.

May God be glorified through your input into my life and these pages!

Table of Contents

Contents (Continued)

Preface

This is the book I thought I would never write. Not because I don't know enough about the subject, but because I felt I was disqualified to write about sexual purity.

As a single divorced male, I engaged in a sexual lifestyle that was promiscuous. I have been places and done things that I wish I had never done. I have images in my mind I wish were not there. I have engaged in activities that wounded other people emotionally and that wounded myself. I did not live a life of sexual purity during those years so I never thought I would be someone to write on this subject.

But I was challenged to write this book by men and women who know me and who know my heart. I could not argue with their insistence that God uses our deepest personal wounds to minister to other wounded people. We all have a wisdom that comes from our wounds, our mistakes, our sins. When we allow God to bring us to repentance and we experience His healing and comfort, we are enabled by His grace and mercy to minister to other people in the same way the Lord has ministered to us.

> When we allow God to bring us to repentance and when we experience His healing and comfort, we are enabled by His grace and mercy to minister to other people what we have learned.

I call this work of God His "recycling mercy." God heals us so He can minister His purposes and grace through us to other hurting people. He recycled Moses, using a forgiven murderer to lead His people out of Egypt and through the wilderness for forty years. He recycled King David, using an adulterer and murderer to become a "man after His own heart" (I Samuel 13:14). God even used David to write some of the most beautiful and powerful passages ever penned by man.

God recycled Peter to lead the Apostles and to begin

to establish the early Church. He recycled a murderous zealot Saul into Paul, the Apostle to the Gentiles. I am convinced that God loves to recycle those people who turn to Him in repentance, and I believe history is filled with stories of these recycled people. I am one of many who has been recycled by a loving and merciful God.

In this book, by His grace, I offer to you some of the wisdom that God has built into me. He gets all the credit. If what you read in these pages helps you, then give God all the credit and certainly all the glory.

Waylon Ward

Introduction

This book grew out of a "Men & Sexual Purity" Seminar I conducted in late 2003. I was asked to share some insights with a group of men who had been working on men's issues and sexual purity. I developed some of the concepts that I had learned in dealing with my own sexual issues and added insights gleaned from 39 years of ministry and more than 50,000 hours of counseling. The seminar was wonderfully successful.

One of the leaders of the men's group came to see me the next week. He brought with him a sack full of books. In the sack were the best books available for individuals on sexual purity. As he laid these out on the table one by one, he explained that he had been struggling with sexual addictions for over six years. As he laid each book down, he commented on what had been helpful in the book and how much this or that seminar had cost. He went through most of the books and seminars that have been available nationally to address sexual issues and addictions for men. He said he did not know how much money he had spent trying to get help with his addiction.

> Our sexual lives have a greater purpose in God's plan than personal pleasure.

Then he did something that surprised me. He reached back into the sack, pulled out the outline to the "Men & Sexual Purity" Seminar and said, "Waylon, this is the best material on this subject I have ever seen!" He suggested that I develop this material and offer more seminars and even write a book on the subject. So the concept for **Sex Matters** was born.

My purpose in developing this material entitled **Sex Matters** is to create a strategy to reframe the way Christians think about sexuality and to encourage sexual purity in the lives of Christians. My desire is to teach Christians about God's purposes for sexuality and how our sexual lives have a greater purpose in God's plan then personal pleasure.

Christians who understand God's Purposes, His Design and His Desires for sexuality, have a stronger motivation to live a life of sexual purity. When they are taught that God will enable them to live lives of purity then many Christians can and will find a new freedom in their personal lives. God enables us to say "Yes" to His higher purposes and gives us the desire and ability to live a pure life.

The need in the sexual area is not about more education concerning biological factors or how to keep buttons buttoned and zippers zipped. There is a crying need to reframe the thinking of the average church member's view concerning sexuality and to help him be transformed from the world's perspective to God's perspective. In order to do this, the attitudes of individual men and women must be transformed as must the attitudes and beliefs of couples and parents.

> **The need in the sexual area is not about more education concerning biological factors or how to keep buttons buttoned and zippers zipped.**

Our culture is sex-saturated. It has become an obsession of the media and millions of people. Millions of lives are being wounded and even destroyed by the rampant sensuality that is being pushed as a "good thing." The Church has become polluted with secret sins. Thousands of Christians, particularly men, are "on the bench" spiritually because of their shame, guilt and regrets. Many people need to find freedom from their addictions, shame, guilt and regret before they can make much progress in reframing their personal perspective of sexuality. Hundreds of pastors have been taken out of the game by their failures in the sexual area. There are too many victims!

I believe that God through Jesus Christ can set people free and that He wants to move in the hearts and souls of Christians to call us back to His desire for purity among His people. By His power and grace, this Sex Matters Strategy will accomplish what He wants it to accomplish.

Part One

Understanding the Battle

Chapter One

"The Battle Is an Inside Job"

Winning the battle against sexual immorality, sexual temptations and learning to express your sexuality in the way God intended is an *inside job*. God wants to change your heart and soul. As you are transformed from the inside out, you will win the battle. God can transform your life. He wants to set you free to live a life of sexual purity.

You don't win with lots of rules about what not to do. This battle cannot be won through the "hollow and deceptive" philosophies of the world that depend on human rules and basic principles of this world (Colossians 2:8, 20-23). Paul says:

"Such regulations indeed have an appearance of wisdom, with their self-imposed worship, their false humility and their harsh treatment of the body, but they lack any value in restraining sensual indulgence."
Colossians 2:25

The life that wins the battle over sexual sin is the life that battles with the faith that God's power enables.

I pray also that the eyes of your heart may be enlightened
in order that you may know the hope to which he has called you,
the riches of his glorious inheritance in the saints,
and his incomparable great power for us who be-lieve.
That power is like the working of his mighty strength,
which he exerted in Christ when he raised him from the dead
and seated him at his right hand in the heavenly realms . . ."
Ephesians 1:18-20

What God wants is not simply external control, but internal integrity and reality. Anyone can "white-knuckle" it

15

for a period of time, but that is not winning the battle!

Winning the battle is freedom because your heart and soul are free from the compulsive pressures of your sexual desires. The temptation to engage in sexual immorality, in your imagination or in your behaviors, is like a bird that flies by, but never lands. Protecting yourself from sexual stimuli is not a constant checklist of "dos" and

> *Protecting yourself from sexual stimuli is not a constant checklist of "dos" and "don'ts".*

don'ts". It is enjoying your sexual feelings and expressions within the bonds of a covenant marriage relationship, knowing the joy of giving and receiving sexual pleasure as part of that relationship. For the single person, it can be the anticipation of a joyful future, blessed by God, as you wait and pray for God to bring you a person to share your life and soul with.

Are Most Christians Winning?

The truth is that many Christians are winning the battle against immorality, but the media and researchers have a way of ignoring personal victories. The majority of Christians, who have a vital spiritual life, are walking in honest openness and purity before God. However, statistics confirm that the Church is filled with many people who are not winning the battle over their sexual compulsions and immorality. There appears to be no higher level of sexual purity in the Church than there is outside the Church. But there is more guilt and shame. I have counseled thousands of Christians wrestling with their compulsions, shame and guilt, and I have seen the devastation caused by sexual immorality in individual lives, marriages and families. I have wrestled with my own sexual compulsions and issues. A spiritual battle rages within the Church. There are many Christian men and women who are winning. But there are also millions who are losing.

Sammy slumped in the chair in my office. He didn't waste anytime:

"My big sin is sex. It is my god. It is an escape. I am a prisoner of sex. I am hooked on sex just as if I were shooting stuff in my veins."

For Sammy, sex mattered very much. He was addicted to his own sexual desires and impulses; he was addicted to the sexual behaviors he engaged in.

Richard was the executive director of a medium size Christian ministry. He had been a pastor, then a marketing person who traveled for the ministry organization. He was in my office because his wife had discovered his promiscuous behavior.

As a young man, Richard had been very active sexually but there was a period, after he married and entered the ministry, when he was able to walk in sexual purity. He told me how his first affair happened while he was pastoring and then how he became addicted to women on his trips. He was now on the verge of losing his wife and family, and his heart was hard and cold.

Sammy and Richard represent the sexual addictions that hide in church pulpits and pews next to the untold thousands of other Christians who struggle weekly, if not daily, with unwanted sexual fantasies, pornography, and masturbation. A well-known author and pastor from one of the largest churches in America said recently that more than 50% of men in the average church struggle with internet pornography. The stain of sexual shame and guilt permeates every area of the Church. This pain paralyzes and eliminates thousands from Christian service and ministry. It seeps over into their family life.

Many parents wrestle with what they should say to their kids and end up saying nothing because they fear the "big question": "Dad, did you and Mom...?" So the critical responsibility of sex education is left to the schools.

Teens engage in sex as normal dating activity and simultaneously participate in church youth functions. Fathers leave a men's meeting at church and then spend two hours online visiting different pornographic web sites. Choir members have affairs with one another, not caring that people in the church may suspect their infidelity. Marriages shattered by adultery are so common that no one seems surprised. Families are broken and destroyed. Hearts are broken.

> *Statistics show that 50% of men in an average church struggle with internet pornography.*

God did not intend the Church to be this way!

The "Pickle Principle"

Consider the "Pickle Principle". You and I have a lot in common with a pickle. Look around and you can see lots of examples of the "pickled-life syndrome." The average church is like a jar of pickles!

> *You and I are a lot like a pickle!*

In order to make pickles, we place cucumbers in a solution called brine, a mixture of vinegar, spices and water. After a cucumber soaks in this brine for a period of time, it is changed and becomes a pickle. The brine changes the nature and character of the cucumber. The cucumber soaks up its environment and is forever changed. You and I are a lot like a pickle.

The sex-saturated culture we live in is like the brine the cucumber soaks in. Our hearts and souls have soaked up the brine and it has changed all of us living in this culture.

Today's culture is a sexualized quagmire of pickled people, people who do not know that the cultural brine they have been soaking in has slowly and subtly changed their very nature and character. The Church is filled with pickled people.

God wants to get you and me out of the brine because we can never win as long as we are soaking in this cultural slime. He wants us out of the brine and into an intimate relationship with Him. God wants to restore our freshness, our nature and character, our very innocence. He wants to create in you and me the nature and character of Christ. The Scriptures say that we are to be transformed by the renewing of our minds (Romans 12:1-2). You and I cannot change as long as we are in the brine. We are all pickles until Christ redeems us!

The good news is that God can "un-pickle" us and change our character so we will be different from the culture we have been soaking in. This is the way the battle is won!

Ultimate Pleasure

An example of how the world's perspective has impacted our society is the belief that sex is the ultimate pleasure. Through the media and the implied values of the world, we have been taught that sex is the highest form of pleasure. Hollywood and X rated movie producers would want all of us to believe that there is no greater pleasure available, and that it is the right of every individual, even teenagers, to have this pleasure. Malcolm Muggeridge wrote, "The orgasm has replaced the cross as the focus and the image of fulfillment."

> *"The orgasm has replaced the cross as the image of fulfillment."*

Sexual orgasm is a beautiful, although brief, pleasure, but is it the greatest of all pleasures? It certainly is a physical high, a blast of sensual delight, but is it the best and highest of all pleasures that should define a person's life? No one would deny that a sexual orgasm feels good, but if the pleasure is only physical, can it really be the greatest and highest pleasure? When sexual orgasm is degraded to a purely physical experience, it loses the intense joy of a lasting commitment, an enduring companionship, the joy of family life, and the wonderful mystery of spiritual union. To make sex the greatest of all pleasures is to degrade the human experience to the same level of instinctual activity of all other animals.

> *To make sex the greatest of all pleasures is to degrade the human experience.*

You cannot segment sex from relationship and call it the highest pleasure, the greatest of human experiences. Most of the youth and the majority of adults in this culture have been pickled into the pursuit of sex as the ultimate pleasure. This is the power of the cultural brine.

"We are half-hearted creatures, fooling about with drink and sex and ambition when infinite joy is offered us, like an ignorant child who wants to go on making mud pies in a slum because he cannot imagine what is meant by the offer of a holiday at the sea. We are far too easily pleased."

C.S. Lewis

Another aspect of this pickling process is the belief that no one has the right to deprive another person of this greatest of all human pleasures, that no one has the right to tell anyone else what is right or wrong about the expression of his/her sexuality. This is part of the brine that has permeated even the Church. Another issue involves the right of every person to enjoy sex as soon as they become physically mature.

20

The world's views and beliefs have opened up the door for factors that will destroy healthy relationships and families.

Tim Stafford wrote in his book, The Sexual Christian, that there was a time when people could go through the day without seeing or hearing any mention of sex. But today is different. Stafford writes,

"We live in a constant bath of depersonalized, imaginary, highly provocative sexuality. To the modern person this seems normal, he is barely aware of it."
Tim Stafford, The Sexual Christian

The World's Perspective vs. The Christian Perspective

The Christian perspective of sexuality stands in direct opposition to the pickling brine of the secular world's perspective. No one should be surprised that this is true. The secular world has always thought the Christian view was prudish, naive and repressive. How do these two differing perspectives vary?

The secular world's view, as is commonly expressed through the media and even by many researchers and educators, is that the purpose of sexuality is primarily pleasure. Society acknowledges that procreation is an aspect of sexual relations, but that primarily it is a right of all humans to enjoy and experience the pleasure of their sexuality.

> *Every individual is a living soul, created by God to be in relationship with Himself.*

Pleasure is seen by most as the goal of all sexual expressions. If two consenting individuals desire to experience the pleasure of sexual relations in any particular form they choose and if it does not hurt anyone else, they should be

21

free to connect and enjoy such pleasure.

When individuals make sexual encounters only a physical, pleasurable activity and remove the emotional, spiritual and relational components, they rob the sexual encounter of all its mystery and sacredness. If pleasure is the purpose and goal, then the other person is just an object to be used for sensual gratification. Every individual is a living soul created by God to be in relationship with Himself. Persons have great value and, when they become objects for sensual purposes, it is degrading.

The Christian perspective is that the purpose of sex is relational with pleasure being the by-product. The key difference concerns the priority of committed relationships. God created sex as the highest relational experience a couple can know in this world, a way for a man and a woman to bond and connect in a covenant marriage relationship. This relational covenant and connection is for creating a family built on the foundation of that relationship. In this connected and committed family, children can grow into healthy adults. The sexual relationship was designed to provide unity, love and pleasure for the husband and wife and to preserve this family unit. The purpose for sex was first and foremost relational with pleasure being the added bonus.

The secular world's perspective and the Christian perspective both produce logical, but different, attitudes and outcomes from sexual activities. If you chart the various aspects of these two perspectives, it looks like this:

Secular World Perspective	Christian Persepective
Sex is for pleasure.	Sex is for intimate relationships in marriage.
Sex focuses on the body.	Sex focuses on the person.

Secular World Perspective	Christian Perspective
Persons become objects to be used for pleasure.	Persons are valued and experience intimacy with their partner.
Attitude is one of taking/using.	Attitude is giving/receiving.

Consequences are destructive for both partners.
  Partners feel used.
  Partners feel guilt
  Self-esteem is lost.
	Consequences are enriching and healing for both partners:
	  Partners feel loved.
	  Partners feel affirmed.
	  Self-esteem is enhanced.

God's purpose/goal for sex is intimacy in the marriage relationship with pleasure being a wonderful by-product. Sex by God's design is about relationship much more than pleasure.

The Real Problem

The real problem with the secular worldview of sex is that it separates sex from the human heart. The world's strategy is designed to create a situation in which a person can have sexual pleasure without risking his heart. God's perspective is that, by design, you cannot separate sex from your heart and soul.

> *God is the Great Connector and Satan is the Great Disconnecter.*

The Scriptures say that sexual immorality comes from the heart. So do lasting sexual relations in a covenant marriage. When God changes a person's heart, He makes it possible to love from the heart.

23

This is the key to loving relationships.

Relationships are vital to understanding God's Kingdom and His view of all the aspects of human experience and existence. It is important you remember that God is the "Great Connector" and Satan is the "Great Dis-connector". The World's view ultimately disconnects and destroys individuals, relationships and families. The Christian view connects individuals in loving committed relationships and creates healthy marriages and families.

Remember John 10:10: (parentheses added)

"The thief (Satan) comes only to steal and kill and destroy; I (Jesus) have come that they (you) may have life, and have it to the full (may enjoy it)."

The message of Christianity is not how bad the secular world's view is; the message is that there is so much more. A Christian perspective of sex offers so much more. God has a better way!

CHAIN BREAKERS

√ Winning the battle is an inside job! God wants to change your heart and soul. As you are transformed from the inside out, you will win the battle.

√ We all live in a sex-saturated, pickling brine that affects the way we think about sex matters. God wants to get us out of the brine because we can never win as long as we are soaking in this cultural slime. He wants us out of the brine and into an intimate relationship with Him.

√ The sexual relationship was designed to provide unity, love and pleasure for the husband and wife and to preserve the family unit. The purpose for sex was first and foremost relational with pleasure being the added by-product.

Chapter Two

"Why Does Immorality Hurt So Much?"

How can you gain an understanding of your sexuality? How can you learn to express it and control it according to God's plan? Is it possible for you as a Christian to integrate into your life a proper relational view of sex without yielding to seductive temptations? The answer is a resounding "yes"! By understanding God's purposes for sex and by recognizing His Design and Desire for sexual human beings, you can have a bigger reason for your personal purity. You can discover His relational intent in healthy sexuality, and you can discover the richness and joy of human sexuality as God intended it to be. You can win the battle!

Sex Matters

Sex does matter. Whether sex is the wonderfully exquisite experience of an older couple in marriage, the sweet mystery of a young teen's first sexual arousal or the shameful secret of an individual plagued by unwanted sexual temptations . . . sex matters! For everyone it matters and it matters how you view sex and how you express yourselves sexually. Exquisite joyfulness, mysterious pleasure, shameful disgust and thousands of additional expressions written about sensuous sexuality through the ages all communicate that sex matters.

> *Nothing in your human experience cuts such a wide swath through the realm of your emotions as does your sexuality.*

Sex can be a joyful experience of human connecting and it can be a painful horrible atrocity. And the same person at different times can experience either the joy or the pain. Nothing in your human experience cuts such a

27

wide swath through the realm of emotional experiences as does your sexuality. In today's world, nothing touches every possible emotion humans are capable of like sensuous sexuality (sex with pleasure as the focus) does. We live in a sex-saturated society.

There has never been a time in the history of this country when sexual activities are so openly discussed, when people know more about the biology of sex or when it has been such a topic of public debate. And never has there been a time in history when so many people have been hurt, wounded or destroyed by sexual activities. It appears that frank openness and public awareness have not created greater joy, but rather a deeper despair and more dysfunctional relationships. We seem to have more education, but less character.

Can Education Build Character?

Christians, like so many others in the world, are slow to realize that education alone does not create character. The open freedom to talk about and to engage in sexual activities, the more educated people have become and the more experiences people have had, have not created healthier relationships and certainly not healthier families. Education does not enable a person to live an ethical, loving life. Maturity of character is not the product of education alone. It is the result of relational experiences where parents model and live a life of character. Without a basis for determining what is right or wrong, character loses its meaning.

> Without a basis for determining what is right or wrong, character loses its meaning.

Without a generational transfer of values and morals based on an absolute standard, today's young people are like ships without a rudder. Today's cultural brine does not

28

build mature character. It does just the opposite.

Some people would argue that the current atmosphere of sensuality is an improvement for society, but the impact of sexually transmitted diseases on human health, the increasing number of broken hearts and families, the increasing amount of sexual abuse and dozens of other

> *Today's young people are like ships without rudders.*

issues in society would argue strongly that increased sensuality is not a good thing for the human race.

Society and even the Christian Church are being destroyed through this epidemic of sensuality. We should be shocked by the callous exhibition of sensuousness in every corner of our society and be deeply troubled when we see the same callous insensitivity permeating the Church. Traditionally the Christian faith has been at odds with the world, particularly in the sexual arena. Christians have been taught to be in the world but not of the world: to be salt and light, holding up a higher moral standard than what the world exhibits. Today, Christianity has lost that distinction. As Dr. Howard Hendricks says, "In the midst of a generation screaming for answers, Christians are stuttering."

Why Do Sex Sins Hurt So Much?

The same sexual feelings that bring joy to a husband and wife bring pain, guilt and shame to people when they give themselves over to sensuality outside of God's plan. A young woman tries to commit suicide from the guilt. A young man in his twenties, eaten up by guilt and shame, mutilates himself by trying to amputate his own penis. No one knows how many thousands of people act out the shame and guilt and regret that they have experienced because of sexual immorality. How much emotional pain have sexually transmitted diseases caused? How can we measure the heartbreak and devastation caused by abortion? How much of the guilt, shame and pain about sexual immorality and abuse fuels the epidemic of addictions in society?

Thousands of people are hurting and feeling shame and guilt from sexual behaviors outside of God's ordained purposes. The counseling offices and Pastor's studies are filled with these people. Pastors and counselors will tell you that there is a greater intensity of shame and pain in the people they counsel when the issues involve sexual sins. No other sin creates the same sense of pain, shame and guilt. Sexual sins stain your soul at a much deeper level than any other sin. Paul wrote in I Corinthians 6:18 that all other sins a man commits are outside his body. Sexual sin touches you deep in your heart and soul. Sexual activities outside of God's ordained purposes leave severe guilt and shame wounds particularly for Christians.

> *Sexual sins stain your soul at a much deeper level than any other sins.*

Why Does Sexual Immorality Wound and Damage People at Such a Deep Level?

- Sexual immorality is inside the body. This is what Paul was referring to in I Corinthians 6:18. The body is the container for the soul. A person is a living soul with skin on. What happens outside the body may somewhat impact the soul of the person, but sexual involvement always touches the soul. Sexual sins stain the soul like no other sin does.

- Sexual immorality attacks and contaminates the roots of your self-identity. When you base your worth and value on another person's response to you, the foundation of your self-worth is on shaky ground. You were created as a male or as a female and you are designed to base your self-identity on what God says about who you are, not on the responses of other human beings. When you involve yourself in sexual activities outside of God's design, you become vulnerable to another person's evaluation of you in the most intimate of ways. Sexual activities and passions outside of God's ordained purposes undermine the very foundations of who you are as a man or as a woman and establish your source of identity in sensual pleasure instead of a loving Creator.

- <u>Sex sins expose and exploit your deepest emotional and spiritual vulnerabilities.</u> In the counseling office, individuals rarely if ever weep scalding tears about any other sense of loss like they do for a sexual relationship when it ends. There are soul ties that bind two partners together in unseen ways and there is a sense that part of you has been stolen. There is a hole in your

> *Sex sins beat you up emotionally like no other sin because they touch the whole person and not just your body.*

soul where the connection was ripped from you. Thousands of people ache and cry with regret and shame and devastation from these sexual relationships outside of God's plan. Some cry because they were violated, others because they willingly participated and invited someone into their heart and soul, others because they were perpetrators.

Sex sins touch the human soul like no other sin can or does. A person's deepest soul wounds are exploited. Childhood deprivation is used to seduce. Deepest passions are exposed and aroused. Sex sins beat you

31

up emotionally like no other sin because it touches the whole person and not just your body.

• <u>Sex sins have a unique ability to create a deep sense of shame and guilt.</u> This guilt and shame robs you of your boldness and confidence because it is one of Satan's favorite tools. Nothing keeps you from sharing your faith or ministering and counseling one another like the remorse over sex sins. Why is this so? Because the shame, guilt, and regrets are deeply internal, not just surface pains. Because sex involves the whole person, your heart and soul are contaminated, not just your body.

• <u>Sex sins compromise the deepest human covenant relationship: marriage.</u> It is fairly obvious how adultery betrays the marriage covenant, but so does sex before marriage. Sex sins poison the trust and personal confidence in your partner as well as within yourself when you know you were active sexually with each other or before you met each other. Satan makes sure this distrust eats away at the safe feelings of not being compared. Shame and guilt about your personal history can paralyze your ability to freely give yourself to your partner in marriage. And many times there is a fear of your own ability to not succumb to temptations and go outside the marriage for sex. You could not control yourself before marriage, why do you think you can now in marriage?

> *Only men and women are endowed with the ability to produce another living soul. Satan cannot. No wonder he hates humans!*

•<u>Sex sins strike at the most sacred ability that God gave humanity when He created men and wom-</u>

32

en in His image: the ability to create and produce living souls. Humans can beget life. Angels cannot. Satan
cannot. Only men and women are endowed with the
ability to produce another living soul. No wonder Satan hates humans! No wonder he tries to destroy the
family and uses sex as his favorite tool. He strikes at
that part of you that reminds him of what he does not
possess and that part of you that is most like the Creator. You and your spouse can create life, and anything
that has the potential to destroy that ability touches
your deepest fears and pain.

No wonder sex sins feel so bad. Sex sins slash at
your heart and soul as no other sin. But there is a solution! Understanding God's design and purposes and
living within His boundaries can eliminate most of the
fear and struggle with your sexuality.

(**Note:** I am indebted to Pastor Jack Hayford for the seed
thoughts behind this material. His tape "Why Sex Sins
Are Worse Than Other Sins" was most helpful.)

CHAIN BREAKERS

√ By understanding God's purposes for sex and by recognizing His Design and Desire for sexual human beings, you will have a bigger reason for your personal purity.

√ Sexual immorality will take you further than you want to go, keep you longer than you want to stay and cost you more than you want to pay. But you can choose not to go there!

√ Living within the boundaries that God has set for us can eliminate most of the fear and struggle with our sexuality.

Part Two

Understanding Our Sexuality

Chapter Three

"God's Wonderful Idea"

"Sex within marriage was given that human loneliness might end."
John White, Eros Defiled

God's Original Idea: Sex

When you read the account of the creation in the first three chapters of Genesis, you can begin to understand some basic truth about your sexuality.

- <u>Sex is God's idea.</u> He thought up the very complex idea; He designed all the body parts and He designed them each to work as they do. He created all the hormones and He decided how they would all work together in ways science still has not figured out. He intended sex to be a wonderful, even mysterious, part of human experience (Proverbs 30:18-19).

  "The physical pleasures of sex are God-given. Your body has the capacity to be deliciously stimulated because God made it so. Pleasures, as C.S. Lewis once pointed out, 'is God's invention not the devil's."
  John White, Eros Defiled

- <u>By God's design, sex is not simply about human bodies.</u> It is about human souls interacting with each other. A human being is "a soul with skin on". A soul does not exist in this world separate from a body and a living body always has a soul. What happens to the body happens to the soul in that body.

- <u>Human sexuality is different from sex among animals.</u>
  o Humans have a choice about when, where and with whom they engage in sexual activities. Humans are

not ruled by instincts.

o Humans usually prefer to have sexual activities in privacy.

o Humans are the only species that usually have sex face-to-face, which emphasizes the relational aspect of human sexuality.

o Humans are one of the few species that have sex for reasons other than procreation. Humans have sex often when procreation is not a purpose.

o Humans usually have a prior contract, verbal/ written/financial, before they engage in sexual activities. When they do not have some kind of contract, it is called abuse or rape.

Human sexual experience is designed by God to be a whole person experience. It involves the body, soul and spirit which makes it powerful, beautiful and mysterious. Within God's purposes, sex can be sacramental. When it is experienced outside God's ordained purposes, it is wounding and hurtful.

> *Humans are the only species that usually have sex face-to-face.*

Divine Purposes in our Sexuality

Sex is not a curse to be endured. God is not down on sex. One of Satan's great lies that permeates our culture is that God is down on sex, that the Christian perspective robs individuals of their God-intended rights. It is the familiar line used with Eve: "Did God really say…" (Genesis 3:1). The Biblical view of sexuality is a beautiful picture of relational sexual experience that enables its readers to have the real story about sexuality.

From the Scriptures, it is possible to develop five distinct purposes for sex interwoven like a beautiful tapestry. Having God's purposes as the foundation for your understanding will enable you to reframe your sexual experiences and assist in delivering you from the pickling influence of the culture.

Purpose One: Procreation

God commanded His creation to "be fruitful and multiply." (Genesis 1:28; 9:1) To date, man has no other way of fulfilling this command than through sexual intercourse. Some might hope that the idea of "test tube" babies will be a new way to fulfill the command, but realistically most sensible people agree that the chances of test tube babies becoming the norm instead of the exception are

> God is not down on sex! It was His idea to begin with!

highly unlikely. God knew what He was doing when He designed the procreation process and endowed it with the by-products of warmth, intimacy, love and pleasure. As long as man has free will, he will choose the route of sexual intimacy for reproduction. This is the first purpose for sex given in the Scriptures. Procreation is a purpose, but it is not the only purpose!

Purpose Two: Unity

The Scriptures indicate that sex was designed by God to be a relational experience to produce unity between a man and a woman in marriage. The male and female become "one flesh" (Genesis 2:24) through sexual intercourse.

The Meaning of "One Flesh"

Scholars do not know and cannot agree as to all that

this idea of "one flesh" means. Most people recognize that it indicates a deep connectedness and unity in the marriage relationship. Both in the Old Testament (Genesis 2:18-24) and the New Testament (Ephesians 5:31-32) this concept is tied intimately to the marriage relationship. Paul ties "one flesh" directly to the sex act in I Corinthians 6:16 which indicates that sexual intercourse, even outside of His purposes, involves a deeper connection of more than just bodies.

Many Christians feel that the concept of "one flesh" is closely linked to the fact that humans are created in God's image, the male carrying in some way the masculine characteristics of the nature of God and the female carrying in some way the feminine characteristics of the nature of God. When they marry and their souls touch in sexual intercourse, they become "one flesh."

> *"The Judaic creation account states that before Eve was take from Adam's body, Adam was created both make and female in the image of God (Genesis 1:27). The two, taken together, compose God's image. (The marriage state, in the Judeo-Christian tradition, is a symbolic restitution of this..."*
> Leanne Payne, *Crisis in Masculinity*

In this deep inner and outer connection, of spirit, soul and body, the two most clearly present the true nature of God and all of His multifaceted attributes and characteristics, a blend of the masculine and feminine.

> *"Something of God is seen in Adam and Eve. As Adam could delight in Eve because she was like him, God finds particular delight in this man and woman because together they are like him. There is fellowship among the three. This is the fundamental idealism of sexuality that Eden introduced."*
> Tim Stafford, *The Sexual Christian*

It is in this intimate connection that the gift of human creativity is expressed through conception. The "one flesh" takes on new meaning as the male and female share life together, including the task of creating new persons.

The "one flesh" concept is part of the mystery of human sexuality that gives sexual experience its deep spiritual meaning. Indeed, sex within God's plan can be sacred and sacramental. This is one of the reasons God set boundaries to human sexuality.

Biblical Marriage

A covenant marriage relationship is the primary boundary established by God. He intended for human sexuality to be expressed only within this committed relationship. The Bible gives some stipulations for a relationship between a man and a woman before it is to be identified as a marriage. These stipulations include:

1. Contractual commitment (a covenant) before witnesses.
2. Companionship (bonding through living together, experiencing life together).
3. Consummation (intercourse). Sexual intercourse consummates the marriage, making it legal and seals the contract.

(**Note**: For more information on marriage in the Bible, see *The New Bible Dictionary and Unger's Bible Dictionary*.)

If an arrangement between a man and a woman does not include these three things, it is not considered a marriage. It does not constitute what God intends a Biblical marriage to be. Marriages are to picture something beyond the horizontal connection of two persons. They are to be a sign of God's bonding to mankind.

"...marriage is a temporary fact of existence on earth and cannot be best understood as an end in itself. It is not a mere convenient compromise either. Marriages are important to God, not simply for the happiness they can bring, but because they point beyond themselves. Marriage is not God's kingdom, but it teaches us what His kingdom is like.
Tim Stafford, The Sexual Christian

The significance of marriage as a picture of God's bonding to mankind can be seen clearly in the Hebrew wedding ceremony and shows why unity through sexual intercourse is an important picture of God's connection to us.

Jewish Wedding Celebrations

The Jewish wedding ceremony at the time of Jesus' life on earth was quite different from wedding ceremonies in this culture. (Jesus attended such a wedding and it is recorded in John 2:1-11.) Instead of the twenty-minute quickie ceremonies so common today, the Jewish weddings often lasted for days, even up to two weeks, and were great feasts and celebrations. At the proper time in the celebration, the bride and groom came before their parents and guests and were given a marked piece of white cloth. This public presentation of the bride and groom reminded all ·in attendance of the significance of marriage and the role of sex in God's design. The community affirmed the importance of the consummation and what it pointed to, God's bonding with His people. The couple were sent away into a pre-selected secluded bridal chamber. They would have intercourse and, as the woman's hymen was ruptured, they would catch the blood and semen on the piece of white cloth. After an appropriate amount of time, the couple would reappear at the wedding celebration to present the marked cloth to their parents. Then the guests would really begin to celebrate!

This marked piece of cloth was known as the woman's "token of virginity" (Deuteronomy 22:31-32). It demonstrated that she was undefiled (a virgin) and that the marriage had been consummated through intercourse. Without consummation, the couple were not legally married. (For a discussion of the Hebrew wedding ceremony see the topic "Marriage Customs" in the article on Marriage in the New Bible Dictionary.)

> **Sex is one condition of a valid marriage covenant.**

Sex was designed by God to produce a special unity in the marriage relationship and is one condition of a valid marriage covenant.

Purpose Three: Love and Pleasure

The third purpose for sex is love and pleasure in the marriage relationship. This purpose in God's plan can be developed from several passages of Scripture in the Old Testament. You can see that God designed sex to enhance the marriage relationship by producing love and pleasure in the intimacy of the relationship, and Old Testament believers enjoyed this blessing in their marriages.

Romantic poetry, sensuous love songs and tender relationships have charged the imaginations of young and old since the beginning of time. The Hebrews have the beautiful Song of Songs that tells the story of Solomon's love for Shulamith, a story so sensual and erotic that young Hebrews were not allowed to read it. Dr. Craig Glickman, in his

> **God is in all true love we experience in this world.**

wonderful book, *Solomon's Song of Love*, captures the beauty of this 3,000 year-old love story as he provides an accurate interpretation of the Song of Songs. It is easy to understand why many call it the greatest love song ever written.

Glickman ties the ancient song to contemporary music and movies to inspire his readers to once again discover that God is in all true love we experience in this world. He quotes C. S. Lewis to help his readers focus on true love:

> *"When we see the face of God we shall know that we have always known it. He has been…within all our earthly experiences of innocent love. All that was true love in them was, even on earth, far more His than ours, and ours only because His."*

C.S. Lewis, *The Four Loves*

In contemporary culture, the goal or purpose of sexual contact has become sensuous pleasure, not intimacy in the relationship. This is exactly the opposite of what God intended. He designed sex to produce and enhance relational intimacy, with pleasure being the added bonus. Too often Christian couples have been pickled and have allowed the secular world's purposes, not God's purposes, to guide their sexual activities. God gave humans the gift of sex to enhance and enrich the marriage relationship and, as the marriage relationship becomes more intimate, the experience of sexual pleasure becomes more intense.

> **As the marriage relationship becomes more intimate, the experience of sexual pleasure becomes more intense.**

In the act of sex, a couple experiences a unique and intense self-awareness and degree of unity and intimacy that is generated by the verbal, emotional, physical and spiritual interaction between them. Each individual senses that he or she, as a whole person, is pleasurable to his/her partner. They sense it is not just "part" of his/her body that gives pleasure. Their total person is loved, appreciated, and enjoyed, not just the experience of sensual pleasure in their bodies. As they connect with their bodies they become aware of their spirits and souls touching in sweet mystery. It is as if the partners picture God to each other with each giving total love, unconditional acceptance and delight.

Sensuous Saints in the Old Testament

There is abundant evidence in the Scriptures that Old Testament believers enjoyed their sexuality as God intended. Sensual pleasure was to be an important by-product of sexual intercourse in a couple's marriage relationship. Consider a few passages that demonstrate the pleasure God intended for couples to experience in their married sexual experience.

- Moses writes in Genesis:
  To the woman He said, "I will greatly multiply your pain in childbirth, in pain you shall bring forth children; yet your desire shall be for your husband, and he shall rule over you."
  Genesis 3:16

  God used the word "desire" when He spoke to Eve about the consequences of her sin. This word means sexual drive or passion, and the context indicates that Eve would seek her husband for this pleasure. The implication of this passage is that sex is a pleasurable passion ordained by God. The pain of childbirth will be forgotten and the woman's sexual desire will remain for her husband.

- Another passage that enlightens readers to the sexual pleasure God provided for couples in marriage is in Genesis 18:12. This verse is from the context of Abraham's visit from the Lord at the Oaks of Mamre. These

45

visitors inform Abraham that Sarah, his wife, will have a son. Sarah was standing outside the door of their tent and the author records what happened:

So Sarah laughed to herself as she thought, 'After I am worn out and my master is old, will I now have this pleasure?'

Genesis 18:12

Sarah did conceive and have a son as God had promised, but for this study the word "pleasure" has significance. In the original language it is a word that often refers to pleasure involved in the gratification of sexual desire. Sarah laughed at the thought that she and Abraham would have intercourse and enjoy sexual pleasure again so she might have a child. She did not believe it was possible, either to have that pleasure or to get pregnant at her age. This godly woman, who is held up as an example to wives everywhere (1 Peter 3:6), acknowledged that she had sexual pleasure with her husband.

• From the recorded history of Isaac and Rebekah, there is another passage of Scripture that indicates the pleasure God allowed and intends in sex. Isaac and Rebekah lived in the land of Gerar. Isaac, out of fear, had Rebekah pretend to be his sister and not his wife. She evidently was so beautiful that Isaac feared the men of this country would kill him so they could take her. So Isaac and Rebekah lived this ploy for many days.

When Isaac had been there a long time, Abimilech, king of the Philistines looked down from a window and saw Isaac caressing his wife Rebekah. so Abimilech summoned Isaac and said, 'She is really your wife!'

Genesis 26:9-9

The king could tell by the "caressing" that Isaac and Rebekah were engaged in that they were not brother and sister. The word literally means in the original language, fondling, playing with. The image conveyed is that they were having fun as they engaged in sexual foreplay.

Many other passages could be cited to demonstrate that pleasure is a God-ordained by-product of sexual intimacy in marriage. For further examples, you might investigate Deuteronomy 4:5 ("happiness" literally means sexual pleasure), Proverbs 5:18-19, and the Song of Songs. The Song of Songs is a beautiful picture of married sexual love and was added to the Scriptures to picture for believers God's great desire for His Bride the Church.

> *Song of Songs is a beautiful picture of married sexual love.*

It is the story of the marriage of God to His people. It is the story of romance and passion as Solomon and his "bride" move from courtship to marriage.

The conclusion any reasonable student of the Bible can reach is that sex is to be a pleasure in marriage, not a penalty. God created the idea of sexual interaction to enhance the love relationship in marriage and to produce pleasure in the couple's intimacy.

In the first three purposes we have discussed procreation, unity, love and pleasure. We have seen how sex is designed to give worth and value to both partners. This leads us to…

Purpose Four: Enhancement

The fourth purpose for sexual involvement is to enhance the spiritual and emotional self-esteem of each partner. Pastors and counselors have observed how God uses sexual intimacy in marriage to enhance the spiritual and emotional development of both husband and wife. This purpose can be drawn from all the teachings in the Bible on sex. The male experiences the essence of his masculinity and is made to feel more masculine in a healthy sexual relationship in marriage. A woman experiences the essence of her femininity and is made to feel more feminine in a healthy sexual relationship in marriage. Both partners have their self-image affirmed and built up in loving intimacy. The emotional power of unconditional love and acceptance, lived out in a long term, committed covenant relationship, can never be overstated.

The commitment in marriage, as husband and wife feel

> *God designed sex to enhance the spiritual and emotional development of both husband and wife.*

loved as a whole person, makes the sexual relationship healing to their personalities. They are freed from comparison, competition and fear. They are able to relax and grow in the love they experience. People use sex outside of marriage not so much for healing as for anesthetizing the pain of their aloneness and emptiness; however, the loss of personal esteem and self-respect have just the opposite effect. Sex in a marital commitment can be healing and can produce spiritual and emotional growth.

Purpose Five: Prevention of Immorality

A final purpose for sex is that it was designed by God to prevent sexual immorality outside of marriage. Paul says (1 Corinthians 7:1-5) that husbands and wives should fulfill their duty sexually to their mates and thereby assist their partners in maintaining sexual purity and avoiding temptation.

Ideally, both husband and wife should have an equal sexual desire, but in real life this often is not true. This inequity in desire and the issues involved in balancing a busy family life with marital intimacy can be the cause of much frustration and bitterness in marriages.

Paul's writings in this passage have been used as an emotional club in many marriages over the centuries. One partner points out the other's failure to live by what is written, trying to "guilt" the other into sexual activities. Even the fact that this passage has been mentioned may have elevated some of your guilt feelings. This passage was not written to beat you down with guilt, but to give you hope that you, too, can have joy in your marital sexual relationship. As God heals you, your ability to enjoy sexual intimacy will grow. For some of you the scars and bitterness of the past may be so deep that it will take some in-depth personal healing for you to be free. However, many of you can find a new freedom with some basic understanding of your sexuality and healing of your soul wounds.

What about Sex Outside of Marriage?

"Biblical Christianity is hardly weighed down with sexual negatives. The handful in the Bible focus on a single prescription: no sex outside of marriage. Two commands are central: no adultery and no porneia. (Porneia used to be translated 'fornication', but it is now usually translated more generally as 'sexual immorality."
Tim Stafford, *The Sexual Christian*

God has made no provision for sexual activity outside of the covenant relationship of marriage. The question is often asked as to why He did not make any such provision. Again, God's wisdom and understanding are accepted by faith, but here are some of the possible reasons:

• The sex act involves the whole person: body, spirit and soul. It is too important for people to engage in casually because the destiny of the human soul is at stake.

49

"You cannot act as though sex has no great meaning at all. Sex always has deep relational implications. You cannot, Paul says, treat it as mere recreation."
Tim Stafford, *The Sexual Christian*

- The family must be protected. It is not possible to grow healthy persons outside of healthy family relationships. Society is trying to discover ways to grow kids into healthy adults without the family, but it is not working.

- Sex outside of the marriage covenant hurts and destroys human dignity. God wanted to save His people from such consequences and protect them from the shame of competitive comparisons.

"The rule against adultery is a fence around the institution of marriage...that two people who are drawn together from aloneness to a share life...should have no sexual competition or interference."
Tim Stafford, *The Sexual Christian*

"A partner's infidelity is more than just a disappointing choice to prefer another person (for a night or longer), but a stab in the gut. It threatens any relationship, regardless of how loving. It is an action that canno be mediated by good intentions. It betrays the partner who has entrusted life, body and soul to another. It makes him or her into a sexual competitor.
Tim Stafford, *The Sexual Christian*

- Sex outside of marriage destroys the spiritual picture God intended for sex to portray to humans about His relationship with mankind. He is the eternal Bride Groom and the Church is His bride. He intended that the sexual relationship between husband and wife would enable His people to better understand His desire for and delight in them.

- Sex outside of marriage exposes you, your mate, and your children to the dangers of sexually transmitted diseases.

- Sex outside of God's plan robs you of the highest and best God planned for you to experience. It destroys trust. Satan uses sexual passion and hungers outside of God's boundaries to steal your passion and hunger for Jesus. You can't have both…you will yield to one or the other. Where you focus your affections and desires will determine the decisions you make and will impact the destiny of your life!

- Sexual immorality stains your deepest creative gift, the gift to create life. It produces guilt, shame and causes you to lose respect for yourself and for the other person. It has been suggested that Satan uses sex as one of his favorite temptations because he is angry that he cannot create life like humans can. In his anger he wants to destroy your gift of procreation!

Free sex?
Sex in God's economy is never free.
It is supposed to cost you all that you are each
time you engage in sexual relations.
(Read Proverbs 5:15-23; 7:22-27)

(**Note**: Tim Stafford's book, The Sexual Christian, was a book ahead of its time. It was published in 1989, and I am grateful for his ground-breaking work.)

CHAIN BREAKERS

√ Sex is too important to take casually! It involves the whole person: body, spirit and soul. Understanding this can help you reframe your thinking.

√ God put boundaries around sex to protect your family. It is not possible to grow healthy persons outside of healthy family relationships.

√ From the Scriptures, it is possible to develop five distinct purposes for sex interwoven like a beautiful tapestry: (1) Procreation (2) Unity (3) Love and Pleasure (4) Enhancement (5) Prevention of Immorality.

√ Commit yourself to live and express your sexuality within God's purposes.

Chapter Four

"Understanding God's Design"

In order to express and control your sexuality, it is important that you understand God's design and how He planned for you to handle it. Sex was His idea from the beginning. He intended it to be enjoyed and not just endured.

It is a basic principle of life that understanding enables a person to have a greater sense of control. This is true concerning your sexual nature as well. There are certain factors in God's design that you need to understand to give you this sense of control. With this understanding you can then choose intelligently how to express and control your sexuality. Here are the factors to understand:

- The human sex drive is normal, natural and hormonal. By God's design, your sex drive is a mixture of instinctual factors, hormonal factors, relational factors and human volition.

- God designed the human body to respond sexually to physical/emotional closeness. The hormones that trigger sexual responses make up a complex response mechanism and govern the biological and physiological responses.

- The human body, male and female, normally responds sexually to affection and touch. It is important to remember that God designed the human body and created it in such a way that it would react sexually. He designed your body to be sensitive in all the ways it is sensitive to stimulation. The body reacts sexually to stimulation for a variety of hormonal and emotional reasons.

- When your body is stimulated by a hug from your mate, it will react to that stimulation. In fact, your body can react with sexual impulses when you receive warm affection and tenderness from anyone because your body, in and of itself, does not know the difference between one person's touch and another's. The body is not able to and does not make any discrimination of this nature.

- God gave the responsibility for discrimination and volition to the head, not the body. All discrimination is in your head. Your body is controlled by the choices you make with your will. This may be difficult to understand, but it is very important if you are to gain and maintain personal control of your sexuality.

- The body does not discriminate in and of itself. All discrimination and self-control are located above the shoulders.

- This is a reality about the human body that few people stop to consider. Just because your body reacts with sexual impulses to some stimuli does not mean that you have to choose to be sexual with that stimuli. This may well be why there are so many people struggling with sexual perversions: "If my body responds sexually to someone or something, then why not enjoy myself?"

- Your major (most important) sex organ sits on your shoulders! This is where all discrimination about sexual impulses takes place. God in His wisdom placed your volition and discrimination in your brain...between your ears and not between your legs. In your head you make the choices about what to do with your body's sexual responses and impulses.

- Just because you notice someone who is sexually appealing, just because you have sexual impulses or just because you are turned on sexually does not mean you have to act out sexually.

- Humans can choose to not act sexually when they feel turned on sexually. Animals don't get to choose. Animal sex is purely seasonal, glandular, compulsive and instinctual. God designed human sexuality to be under the control of the human will. We humans have the possibility of making sex sacramental if we choose for it to be so.

In summary, you were given a brain so you can control the responses you choose! Sexual self-control is God's ideal and it is possible for all of us.

Choosing Self Control

The human body was designed by God to respond with sexual impulses to warmth, touch, and closeness. It will respond to these stimuli freely, no matter what the source of the stimulation. If the stimulation is from husband to wife, brother to sister, male to male, animal to human, the body knows only one way to respond and that is sexually.

> *God gave the responsibility for discrimination and volition to the head, not the body.*

But God gives us the ability to control our bodies' impulses thorough the use of our will. A person can choose to respond with non-erotic affection by choosing to keep his body under control. In every situation where our bodies' impulses are stirred, we must make a choice to either act on those impulses or to control those impulses.

The significant control factor has to do with our choices. In our brain we choose what we will do with the sexual impulses in our bodies. Will we choose to control these sexual responses or will we choose to act them out? The Biblical ideal is self-control, expressing our sexual impulses and feelings according to God's purposes and desires.

In our culture, the emphasis is on the freedom of a person to express himself sexually whenever and however he desires. The idea today is that if you have sexual feelings and if they don't hurt anyone else, it is good to express them. As a result many Christians are confused. Some Christians, saturated by the cultural brine we live in, have bought into the cultural values while others have reacted in the opposite direction. Some Christians have become severely legalistic about sexual issues. They have developed elaborate systems to strive for control of their body's normal sexual impulses and functions. If Christians understood the natural sexual impulses generated by their bodies, they could choose to control these impulses instead of reacting with self-condemnation.

> **Your major (most important) sex organ sits on your shoulders!**

Good Sexual Impulses

Some Christians have developed the mistaken idea that all sexual impulses not specifically related to their mate are wrong. Many well meaning Christians have condemned themselves, confined themselves, and punished themselves for having sexual impulses. Because they have not accepted sex as a normal drive, much like hunger or thirst, they have been overwhelmed by self-condemnation and guilt. No where in the Scriptures does God say our body should not have sexual impulses, but consistently we are told to maintain self-control (Romans 6:13, Galatians 5:22, I Corinthians 6:12).

Sexual impulses are normal, natural, and God–ordained. Christians should not condemn themselves because their bodies function the way God designed them to function. Denial of sexual impulses is not self-control and it can lead to explosive consequences. It is not what God intended.

Self Control in Eating

Perhaps this concept can be illustrated by using another of the body's normal drives. Can you imagine how guilty you might feel if you had been taught all your life that the only food you were allowed to ever desire or even notice was food served by your mother? You could never be hungry anywhere except in your own kitchen when your mother put food on the table before you.

Imagine how frustrating it would be trying to live in a world full of delicious goodies but trying to keep your self from noticing their existence. Your body's normal hunger impulses and desire for food would cause it to respond naturally to any food that you were exposed to. Just as God meant for you to have self-control over your eating—not deny the "need" for food—He expects you to have self-control over your sexual urges—not deny the sexual drive. You are to enjoy and limit your intake of food through self-control, and you are to enjoy and limit your sexual expression through self-control.

Appreciating God's Creation

All Christian men and women at times have to deal with sexual temptations. It can happen anywhere, at any time and often is unexpected. When they encounter attractive persons they often sense a sexual impulse. No matter how Godly they are, Christians will notice beautiful people.

Men usually have greater difficulty in coping with the external stimuli. Men respond sexually to external visual images and to physical touch more easily than do women. Women are usually more internal and respond to relational trust and caring more than to external images. But both men and woman have to accept the normal God-ordained sexual impulses and choose to control how they express or not express these feelings.

Again this is by God's design. He wants His people to appreciate all of His created beauty. It is legitimate to appreciate the beauty of God's creation, whether it is a beautiful sunset, a beautiful flower or a beautiful person. But each of us, male and female, has the ability to choose what we will do with what we notice. We do not have to pick every beautiful flower we notice. Noticing a beautiful person is not the same as lusting after that person. But any sexual lust is to be controlled in a Godly manner. (Lust will be discussed more fully in Chapters Nine and Ten.)

> **We do not have to pick every beautiful flower we notice!**

A critical factor that you must understand in order to properly express yourself sexually is that the body and its impulses are created by God. The body's response to stimulation is God-designed. His intent for you is to control your bodily responses and channel them in the proper direction. Your body will have impulses and will respond to warmth, affection, and closeness, and your body's impulses and responses are not a sin. The body's function is God ordained and designed by God; the sin is involved in the choices you make. Your body's impulses and responses can be controlled and expressed as God planned or they can be acted out in a sinful manner in violation of God's plan.

> **The body's function is God ordained; sin becomes involved when you make certain choices.**

What We Learn from Our Parents

Another important factor in learning about self-control is to understand what you were supposed to learn from your family of origin. Ideally you were to have learned from your parents about sexuality and sexual responses. Through their teaching and modeling, you were to receive the basics about relational sexuality. In the relationship with your parents, there are two important areas of your personality that must develop for you to have a healthy sexual understanding.

The first of these is your sexual identity. Until a child is approximately three years of age, both parents are seen as nurturing parent figures. About three years of age a child becomes aware of his/her own sexuality. The little boy sees himself as a male like daddy; the little girl sees herself as a female like mommy. As they grow, the parent of the same sex becomes their model. This modeling process really picks up steam when puberty hits and the child moves into the teen years. Boys model after Dad; Girls model after Mom.

> *Without a parent of the same sex for a model and a parent of the opposite sex to affirm the modeling, a child will have some insecurity in his sexual identity.*

As the child's sexual identity becomes clearer in his mind, he begins to check out his development with the parent of the opposite sex. He models after the parent of the same sex, but confirms his successful development by the reactions to him of the parent of the opposite sex. This is an important process in the formation of a healthy sexual identity and self-image. Without a parent for a model and without a parent to affirm the success of the modeling, a child will have some insecurity in his sexual identity.

Erotic and Non-Erotic Love Feelings

The second important area of your personality that develops in your relationship with your parents is the ability to differentiate between erotic love feelings and non-erotic love feelings. A child has undifferentiated love feelings from birth. He does not know how to distinguish the difference between erotic and non-erotic love feelings. He becomes aware at an early age that it feels good to touch his penis. This is the earliest of the erotic feelings.

In a healthy family, the child learns to make the distinction of erotic and non-erotic love feelings through a healthy relationship with the parent of the opposite sex. The child offers all of his love feelings to the opposite sex parent, both the erotic (which is very limited in early childhood) and non-erotic. Little boys freely give all of their love feelings to Mommy; little girls give all of their love feelings to Daddy. In these healthy early childhood relationships, there is lots of healthy affection. The healthy parent returns to the child, through healthy affection and touching, non-erotic love feelings and affection. By design the erotic love feelings are then left undeveloped. They are suppressed and reserved for the adult marriage relationship.

> *The proper non-erotic love relationship with the parent of the opposite sex prepares the child for adult love relationships.*

The proper non-erotic love relationship with the parent of the opposite sex prepares the child for adult love relationships. The child that receives adequate non-erotic affection learns to feel safe and secure in the parent of the opposite sex's arms and will then be comfortable in giving and receiving non-erotic love with his/her friends and peers. They are able to view all relationships from a non-erotic perspective. This safety and security developed in

60

childhood with the parent of the opposite sex makes it safe later for healthy erotic experiences in marriage.

When the child moves into puberty and early teens he/she knows how to relate to the opposite sex with non-erotic love feelings. They have not been deprived of healthy affection so they are comfortable in giving and receiving non-erotic love and affection. When a child has experienced a deprivation of healthy love and affection from the parent of the opposite sex, the child often has unmet emotional needs and wounds. When the love relationship with the parent of the opposite sex is inadequate (not enough love and affection) or improper (parent returns erotic love) the child is unable to make the distinction necessary between erotic and non-erotic love feeling. Parents should never return to their children erotic love feelings or sensations. When they do, it is always abusive and creates deep wounds and severe confusion in the development of the child's healthy sexual function in adult life.

With undifferentiated love feelings, the child grows into a young teen who experiences confusion in interaction with the opposite sex. With the active development of their sexuality at this time and the influence of cultural standards, individuals often become involved in erotic love relationships long before they are ready for marriage. These individuals move into adult life still unable to give or receive love and affection that is non-erotic. All love and affection has sexual implications to them, and they are unable to relate within the Body of

> *With undifferentiated love feelings, a child grows into a young teen who experiences confusion in interaction with the opposite sex.*

Christ or in other adult relationships as God intended. There are thousands of Christians who wrestle with non-differentiation of love feelings every day.

As a result of the problem of undifferentiated love feelings the entire culture swims in a brine of sexual pre-occupation that saturates all of life and hinders the emotional development of individuals.

When a person is raised in this atmosphere, deprived of a proper experience of non-erotic love and affection, he grows up not ever feeling really loved. Non-erotic love satisfies the inner need to be loved in a way that erotic love never can, and non-erotic love accepts the individual as a whole person which erotic love does not. If all the person knows is erotic love, then he falls into the lie that the only thing he has of value to offer another person is erotic love. He never feels that he is loved without strings; he only feels loved when sexual pleasure is given or received. In a healthy marriage, there must be lots of non-erotic love and affection as well as unselfish erotic love and affection.

> *As a result of the problem of undifferentiated love feelings, our entire culture swims in a brine of sexual pre-occupation that saturates all of life and hinders the emotional development of individuals.*

What about the Church?

> *When individuals are able to give and receive healthy non-sexual affection, it has a healing effect on the personality and self-image of both giver and receiver.*

We live in a culture that does not make this distinction between erotic and non-erotic love feelings. Unfortunately Christians have allowed their own love feelings to be distorted in a similar way. In Church culture most touching is distrusted as having sexual implications. If you touch someone, are touched by someone or if you see two people hugging, it is sometimes interpreted as having sexual implications. This is not what God intended, and it was not this way when Jesus walked on the earth.

There is a proper non-sexual affectionate relationship exemplified in the New Testament and experienced by mature Christians in our society today. When individuals are able to give and receive healthy non-sexual affection, it has a healing effect on the personality and self-image of both giver and receiver.

A warm affectionate non-sexual hug says: "You are loved, accepted, and approved. You are worthy and forgiven. I am honored to be your friend." Touching does not always have sexual implications, at least it did not for Jesus and the disciples, and it should not for you.

An interesting Bible study for you would be to study the significance and frequency of touching in the New Testament. You might study Jesus' touching the leper or the blind man, the prostitute washing Jesus' feet or John leaning on Jesus at the Last Supper. Also look at Paul's directives to greet one another

> *The Christian community has been too heavily influenced by the contemporary culture that equates affection and touch with sex.*

with a "holy kiss". While you are studying, look at David and Jonathan's relationship in the Old Testament. You will be surprised at the numerous references to affectionate touching in the Bible. The Christian community has been too heavily influenced by the contemporary culture which equates affection and touch with sex.

Hundreds, even thousands, of Christians are starved for love and affection because they were deprived in their own childhood. Christian parents should give their children lots of healthy non-erotic love and affection while they are young. Perhaps the Church can some day have a generation of adults who have a healthy non-sexual perspective on touching and affection so that the freedom of the New Testament can be restored.

CHAIN BREAKERS

√ God gave the responsibility for discrimination and volition to the head and not the body. All discrimination is in your head and your body is controlled by the choices you make with your will. This may be difficult to understand, but it is very important if you are to gain and maintain personal control of your sexuality.

√ We choose what we will do with the sexual impulses in our bodies, whether to control these sexual responses or to act them out. The choice is ours.

√ Noticing a beautiful person is not the same as lusting after that person.

√ Your major sex organ sits on your shoulders!

√ Learning to distinguish between erotic and non-erotic love feelings helps us be able to give and receive non-sexual affection.

√ Touching is not always sexual.

Chapter Five

"Design Impacts Function and Feelings"

"Gender is a reality and a more fundamental reality than sex…a fundamental polarity which divides all created beings."

C. S. Lewis

God's creative design can be seen in the way He created the male and female anatomy. The study of body structures and how they impact individuals relationally and emotionally is called morphology. God had it all in mind when He created male and female.

Personality and Anatomy

Because of distinct differences in male and female anatomies, there are unique emotional and relational developments in each. Design of the sexual organs has an influence on the personalities of both male and female. This can be observed in several ways.

> The design of the sexual organs has an influence on the personalities of both male and female.

(Note: Many years ago Dr. Maurice Wagner provided the author input for understanding morphology and its impact on the development of the male and female personalities.)

Physiology appears to have a basic effect on thought patterns in the development of a child's personality.

A major difference in effect is due to the fact that a girl is rarely conscious of her major sex organ. She may momentarily become conscious of it at menstruation but she is much less aware of its existence than a boy is of his sex organ. Because of this lack of awareness, a woman

> *Women never "see" their major sex organs so it is less personal.*

can discuss her sexuality more easily than a man can since she is discussing something internal and therefore less personal. She has never seen her sex organ so it is much like talking about her liver or gall bladder.

For men their sex organ is much more real and personal. Men can usually discuss another person's sexuality more easily then they can their own. Because a young boy discovers his penis at a very early age, his primary sex organ becomes very important to him. Because his sex organ is so noticeable and he must handle it daily for urination, a young boy becomes conscious of his maleness early in life. He has a sense of personal pride and self-appreciation as a male that can only be compared to a young girl's feelings about her breasts when she begins to develop as a preteen.

This physiological difference also has an effect on

> *Because his sex organ is so noticeable and he must handle it daily for urination, a young boy becomes conscious of his maleness early in life.*

the person's sexual awareness based on the sensations around the organs. As a boy develops, his sexual feelings are focused on his sex organ. It seems that his body as a whole has less sensitivity to erotic pleasure than does a female's body. A woman's feelings are usually diffused throughout her whole body and only become localized with overt stimulation. For the male his sexual feelings are localized to his genitals.

With an emphasis in today's culture on masturbation, more and more young girls are engaging in masturbation. They are becoming aware of their primary sex organs (clitoris and vagina) at much earlier ages. Some authorities have suggested that this is why teenage girls are becoming

68

more aggressive physically and sexually.

This awareness also impacts a woman's sexuality in that it desensitizes her generalized pleasure feelings and tends to localize these feelings in the genitals. This causes her to have a more singular focus on pleasure instead of the generalized focus God intended. As a result, many of these young women find their sexual responses and pleasures in marriage are not as fulfilling as they might have been.

Because of the God-ordained design of the male sex organ, a boy becomes very aware of sexual stimulation at an early age. He learns what is stimulating and what is not because his sex organ broadcasts loud and clear to him when he is aroused. He is sensitized to touch and sight and becomes aware of erotic stimuli. Sexual sensations and feelings become an important part of his life. A young girl has no overt gauge or signal to call her attention to sexually stimulating situations, therefore she is not as sensitized to the erotic aspects of her environment or her sexual feelings. This difference has a definite effect on the way men and women experience themselves sexually as adults and on their awareness of sexual stimuli in the cultural environment.

What about Circumcision?

In the covenant God made with Abraham, He made circumcision the identifying mark for those who belonged to the one true God. Have you ever wondered why He implemented circumcision as the ritual? He could have branded or marked a man in many other ways and in many other places, so why the penis? I would like to suggest that:

• God knows how important and personal the penis is to the male, so He selected the penis to be where He placed His mark of ownership on His men.

69

- He also knew the struggles men have in the area of sexual self-control so He put a mark on a man's penis to remind him of His covenant with the Lord.

> **Your destiny is in your hands!!**

- Every time a man sees or handles his penis, circumcision is a reminder of ownership …God's ownership of the man and the man's ownership of his own personal destiny. It is to be a reminder that he can choose how to live his life. His destiny is literally in his own hands!

Other Male and Female Differences

Males and females are designed by God to function and respond differently. There is a different vulnerability sexually for the female than for the male. It is a different emotional feeling to be the penetrator as opposed to being the one penetrated. The primary difference appears to be in the need, for the female, of security and safety before she is willing to release her libido. Males, with the different emotions surrounding their ability to be a penetrator, do not struggle with the same fears as does the female. Males are more external in their sexual responses and females are more internal. These differences condition each gender's responses toward life.

Hormonal Differences

There are complex hormonal differences between males and females, and trying to understand them is a very complex task.

> **Testosterone recycles in the male every twenty minutes.**

Basically the female hormonal cycle is a twenty-eight day cycle. The male hormonal cycle is related to testosterone that recycles in the male every twenty minutes. Obviously this is a significant difference and impacts each gender. Since testosterone appears to be the key hormone in both men and women for stimulating sexual desire (the female hormone estrogen is made by the body from testosterone), we should not be surprised that men seem to desire more sexual activity.

Testosterone levels are seasonal, reaching the highest levels in autumn. (That's why we have football in the fall and men's beards get thicker in the fall.) Testosterone levels are highest in the mornings and testosterone is also responsible for men being more hairy, aggressive and competitive.

Another Factor for Men

Males also have another cycle that some men and most women do not realize. This cycle is related to the general function of the male system and is called an "ejaculate build- up." This ejaculate build-up occurs about every 72 hours and creates a physical and emotional tension in most men. As men get older, this cycle slows down but is still noticeable.

> *The ejaculate build-up occurs about every 72 hours and creates a physical and emotional tension in most men.*

The cycle is about every three days for young men; by the time a man is in his sixties the cycle has usually slowed to about once every six or seven days.

With this build-up, men become more sensitized to sexual stimuli; they notice more attractive women and are more prone to lustful fantasies at these times. This tension often interferes with their ability to focus or concentrate at work. Normally this ejaculate build-up is relieved by regular sexual activity in marriage.

For the single guys, the tension can be released through

nocturnal emissions ("wet dreams") or with vigorous exercise. This issue also figures into the struggle many men have with masturbation. (Masturbation is discussed in Chapter Ten.) When a man commits himself to not engage in any sexual activities, not even masturbation, the body cooperates in that this 72-hour cycle slows down. Sexual activity and release stimulates the body to produce more ejaculate. Self-control and abstinence communicates to the body to produce less, so the urgency factor changes. And contrary to popular wisdom, you don't lose it if you don't use it! Remember Jesus was a single adult male so He understands your sexual feelings and even your temptations (Hebrews 4:15).

Bonding Hormone

Another hormone that you might not be familiar with is the neuro-peptide, oxytocin. This hormone is known

> *The bonding hormone, oxytocin, is released in the male each time he ejaculates.*

as the mothering or bonding hormone. Oxytocin is released in the female at the time of the birth of a baby to help bring in her mother's milk and shrink her uterus. It is believed to be a powerful force in bonding the mother with the infant. New research data indicates that oxytocin plays a key role in human romantic attachments, too.

This same hormone, oxytocin, is released in the male every time he has sex. Levels of oxytocin are tripled during erection and orgasm. It is released when he ejaculates, whether it is with his wife, some other person or if he masturbates. Some researchers have concluded that it has a similar bonding effect on the male to his sexual partner as it does with the mother and infant, even calling oxytocin a biochemical "superglue"! It would seem logical that God would build such a hormone into the sex act itself.

Similar research indicates that people who have had multiple sexual partners, becoming bonded to them through sex, diminish the power oxytocin has to maintain a permanent bond in marriage.

It would seem logical that God would build a bonding hormone into the sex act

Counseling experience indicates that married couples who have regular sexual activity have a deeper sense of bonding than do couples that have an infrequent sex life. When couples do not have regular bonding sexually, an emotional drift can set in that hinders intimacy and communication.

(Note: The research information about oxytocin is from an article by Dr. Eric J. Keroack and Dr. John R. Driggs, Jr. of the Medical Abstinence Council.)

Differing Physiologies & Personalities

Physiology has an effect on the differences in thought patterns that develop in the male and female. Since the male organ is designed as an aggressive, penetrating organ, it leads the male toward adventure and excitement. He appears to have a greater desire to challenge, to create, to penetrate the unknown, to discover new things. This desire for discovery and adventure appears to be greater than the average female's desire. Girls are more inclined to nurture, to take care of things, to provide warmth and love. The female organ is a receptive organ designed by God to receive something into it and to create a safe place. She appears to have a greater desire to nurture, to love, to build a nest for her mate and children.

To deny God's ordained design for gender differences is to miss the full richness He intended for His creation.

73

The male appears to experience the essence of his masculinity in dominance and assertion; the female appears to experience the essence of her femininity in loving surrender and nurturing. Man's sense of worth is enhanced by achievements; a woman's sense of worth is enhanced by security, affection, and nurturing. Certainly these tendencies can be overridden but, in general and culturally around the world, these seem to hold true.

> **The woman's responsiveness affirms the man's worthiness.**

These male and female differences need to be seen as part of God's wonderful design. God designed the glory of the female to be revealed through her beauty and ability to create and nurture. The glory of the male is revealed in some adventure through which he demonstrates his strength, agility and perseverance. The women's glory is in her beauty which she unveils through her tenderness, responsiveness and giving of herself to the man. The woman's responsiveness affirms the man's worthiness.

When a woman unveils her physical beauty to her husband, it is a statement of how special he is. If she unveils her beauty to lots of men, it diminishes the uniqueness of her gift. A man demonstrates his glory by coming to the woman and giving himself to her in gentleness and strength, protecting and honoring her and her glory. If he demonstrates this glory to lots of women, it diminishes the uniqueness of his gift.

> **The complimentary structure of the male and female sex organs appears to be matched by complementary components of personality.**

The complimentary structure of the male and female organs appears to be matched by these complimentary components of personality. While different individuals may display some variation of gender differences, to deny what God's ordained design is in structure and development is to miss the full richness He intended for His creation.

"There is profound ontological significance in this matter of essential polarity of the sexes and of the masculine and the feminine genders. To disregard their complementariness out of which issues fullness of being on the natural plane, is finally to strike a blow at the true self in every man—indeed, at being itself."

Leanne Payne, *Crisis in Masclinity*

Morphology Chart

God created two genders with differing physiologies. These different physiologies condition each gender to have different attitudes toward life.

Masculine	Feminine
The primary sex organ is external.	The primary sex organ is internal.
He is conscious of his genitals from early childhood	She is usually not aware of her genitals until puberty.
The penis is more personal for a man. He cannot talk as readily about it.	The vagina is less personal It is almost like any other internal organ (i.e., bladder)

Masculine	Feminine
The penis is an aggressive organ designed to penetrate, point the way, conquer.	The vagina is a receptive organ designed to receive something into it, a space to be filled.
Erotic feelings are more localized.	Erotic feelings are more generalized.
His physiology conditions him to overall be more aggressive in life, to enjoy adventure, exploring, conquering the unknown	Her physiology conditions her to be more nurturing oriented, enjoying more the idea of making a safe, warm place for her family.
Achievement oriented.	Security oriented.
No significant monthly cycle.	Monthly cycle, hormone changes, more conscious of feelings, reproduction, etc.
Stimulated more by sight and touch.	Stimulated more by internal feelings, warmth, security affection, love.
An external gauge to signal sexual excitement which conditions men to be more aware of sexually stimulating sights and circumstances. He is quickly aware of what is stimulating.	Has no external guage to call her attention to sexual stimuli. Aroused slower.

Masculine	Feminine
Fantasies are usually more physical, fantasies of delighting a woman so much she cannot resist.	Female fantasies are more romantic, fantasy of being "swept off her feet."

The tendency of both sexes is to assume the opposite sex feels and thinks the same way he or she does. This is particularly true in romantic, sexual encounters. It is important for men and women to understand that it is a different psychological perspective to be the one who is the penetrator versus the one who is being penetrated.

John Eldredge writes about the sweet mystery and "the way of a man with a maiden" (term used in Proverbs 30:18-19).

"There is something mystic in the way a man is with a woman. Our sexuality offers a parable of amazing depth when it comes to being masculine and feminine. The man offer his strength and the woman invites the man into herself, an act that requires courage and vulnerability and selflessness for both of them....When both of them are living as they were meant to live, the man enters his woman and offers her his strength. He spills himself there, in her, for her; she draws him in, embraces and envelopes him. When all is over, he is spent, but oh what a sweet death it is."

John Eldredge, *Wild at Heart*

CHAIN BREAKERS

√ Understanding God's design enables you to appreciate the opposite sex and maintain sexual self-control.

√ When you understand the way your body responds, you are able to control it and use it to your benefit.

√ God's design gives us a framework within which to live and relate to one another.

√ Thank God for His unique design of each gender. Ask Him to show these unique differences to you in your relationships.

Chapter Six

"A Picture of God's Desire"

God had an additional idea in mind when He created the whole concept of sexual interaction between husband and wife. He desired to make marriage a pattern for the way He relates to His people. He wanted sex to communicate to both partners something about Himself and about the way He relates to each person individually.

The Christian's relationship with God is that of a bride with her husband. This is so hard for us to visualize and understand in our western world. The Jews included Song of Songs in their Scriptures to picture this relationship with God. Spiritually every individual who comes to God is in a feminine receptive posture before God. Each person must have his or her heart penetrated by the love of God. It is in receiving that the new birth takes place in the person's heart and soul.

Sex Pictures God's Relationship with Mankind

In the Bible (Ephesians 5:23-33, Revelation 19:7-8) the Church is pictured as the Bride of Christ. Paul says this is a profound mystery as he writes that husbands are to love their wives as Christ loved the Church. For many people this is a difficult perspective: God desires a relationship with you with the same intensity and love that a young groom has for his bride.

> *Each person must have his or her heart penetrated by God*

As you study the Scriptures and God's interaction with mankind, you can discern that there is a cycle in the love between God and His people. God's love is portrayed throughout the Scriptures as having a certain flow, a pattern to be understood. This pattern of God's love, portrayed in the Old and New Testaments, is to be the same pattern that human married love is to follow. God indicated in the Old Testament that He was wed to the nation Israel. He said He would "betroth" Israel to Himself forever (Hosea 2:19-20). What is this repeated pattern seen in the Scriptures?

In the Old Testament:
- God gives a gift of His unconditional love to His people. It is freely given without any reservation.

- His people receive the gift. (Sometimes they accepted His gift and sometimes they did not trust Him and rejected His gift. When they did not receive His gift, the pattern was broken.)

- His people respond to the gift. When His people received His gift, blessings followed.

- There was rejoicing in the land.

Over and over again, the Old Testament pictures God's pursuing love for His people and their responses. It is a real romance involving a gift being offered and either accepted or rejected.

The pattern is repeated in the New Testament with God's offering of His love gift, Jesus.

- God gives His gift of unconditional love and acceptance (Jesus and His death on the Cross).

- A person receives Jesus into his life.

- That person responds to the gift.

- There is rejoicing by everyone (Luke 15:7,10,22-23). It

says even the angels in heaven rejoice over one person who accepts God's love offered through Jesus.

The pattern is Give, Receive, Respond, Rejoice. The pattern of these four activities can be seen over and over again in God's interaction with mankind.

Marriage Pictures This Pattern

Married sexual love is to mirror this pattern for believers! God's desire is for couples to repeat this pattern in their marriages and be reminded that He ordained marriage for this purpose.

• Each partner gives his/her body as a gift to the other as a demonstration of God's unconditional love.

• Each partner receives the gift offered.

• Each partner responds to the gift received.

• As a couple they rejoice and enjoy pleasure together.

It is God's desire that each partner in the marriage relationship picture God's unconditional love and acceptance to the other partner. Spouses are to picture God's character and unconditional love to each other. This is God's desire for Christian marriage. Each partner is a flesh and blood picture of God's character and attributes. Each partner incarnates God's unconditional love and acceptance and, in this way, the marriage pictures God to the world.

Marriage is intended to fulfill the relational mandate that Jesus gave before He was crucified:

A new commandment I give to you: Love one another. As I have loved you, so you must love one another. All men will know that you are my disciples of you love one another.

John 13:34-35

The Apostle John wrote another passage that can be considered for couples in Christian marriage:

We love because He first loved us. If anyone says, 'I love God.' Yet hates his brother, he is a liar. For anyone who does not love his brother, whom he has seen, cannot love God whom he has not seen. And He has given us this command: 'Whoever loves God must also love his brother.'

1 John 4:19-21

When two Christians understand God's desire that marriage picture His relationship with believers and when they recognize His strategy for married love, it makes for a beautiful marriage relationship.

Husbands, love your wives as Christ loved the Church and gave Himself up for her...

Ephesians 5:25

Paul is saying that you, as a husband, are to picture Jesus' unconditional sacrificial love to your wife. Your hands, your arms, your eyes, your attitudes and behaviors should picture to her what God's character and attributes are like. If you, as the husband, take the lead and picture God the Father's love, grace and mercy to your wife, then she will be encouraged to do the same.

> **Spouses are to picture God's character and unconditional love to each other.**

Peter writes to the wives:

A Picture of God's Desire

Wives, in the same way, be submissive to your husbands...

1 Peter 3:1

Peter is referring to the way Jesus went to the Cross, "by entrusting Himself to the one who judges justly" (I Peter 2:23). Peter is saying to wives that they should reflect to their husbands the same character and attributes that Christ did when He submitted to the Father's will and went to the Cross. Jesus entrusted Himself to the Father by faith when He went to the Cross. Jesus trusted the Father's Word and the Father's character. The wife is to entrust herself to the Father in the same way. As she identifies herself with the Father, she will be able to respond in a Godly way to her husband. She will be able to visualize herself as a picture of Jesus' character and attributes to her husband. Her eyes, her body, her attitudes should picture God's unconditional love and acceptance to her spouse.

> **Jesus trusted the Father's word and the Father's character.**

For this reason a man will leave his father and mother and be united to his wife, and the two will become one flesh. This is a profound mystery—but I am talking about Christ and the church.

Ephesians 5:31-32

God desires for Christian marriage, and particularly the marital sexual union, to picture His relationship with each individual believer and to the Church in general. The sacrificial unconditional love of Jesus is the model for each partner. His picture of service when He washed the Disciples' feet in John 13 should be a great model for BOTH spouses. And since the final evidence given in Scripture of being filled with the Spirit is that of submitting one to another (Ephesians 5:21), spouses should make it their goal

83

to serve one another in unconditional love and acceptance.

Such is God's desire for all Christian spouses. He loves each person unconditionally and He desires each partner to mirror the same kind of love to each other. Give, Receive, Respond, Rejoice…a pattern that will bring rejoicing to your marriage.

Marriage without God is an oxymoron. Marriage was never intended to be experienced apart from the blessings and mercy of God the Father. It is His great portrait of the way He interacts with mankind. What a mysterious and beautiful picture it is.

> *Marriage without God is an oxymoron.*

CHAIN BREAKERS

√ Study what the Scriptures show about God's interaction with mankind. You can discern that there is a cycle in the love between God and His people. This pattern of God's love, portrayed in the Old and New Testaments, is to be the same pattern that human married love is to follow.

> **The Pattern is**
> **Give**
> **Receive**
> **Respond**
> **Rejoice!**

√ Commit yourself to God's pattern and ask God to show you how He desires this pattern to be expressed in your life.

Part Three

Why We Struggle

Chapter Seven

"Understanding the Internal Battle"

Sow for yourselves righteousness, reap the fruit of unfailing love, break up your unplowed ground; for it is time to seek the Lord until He comes and showers righteousness on you.

Hosea 10:12

Could it be that God made sex a difficult battle so we would be forced to break up our unplowed ground to find Him and His provision for our healing and purity?

God does not give us victory easily or quickly in the area of sexual purity. The temptations, the struggles, even the despair of our failures, are all designed to force us to turn to God for the transformation of our souls. God wants us to be more concerned about our relationship with the Deliverer than about being delivered. God is more concerned with inner wholeness that leads to external holiness than He is in just external purity. What God wants is more faith and trust on the inside, not more of our efforts on the outside. God wants to transform our character, not just have us obey through human effort. Holiness includes purity of motive not just purity of behavior.

> God wants more faith and trust on the inside, not more of our efforts on the outside.

Self-control of sexual urges and impulses is possible, but not simply by human effort, constant vigilance, strategies of avoidance, and the scrutiny of accountability partners. These things may prove helpful, but only when our heart motives trust the promises of God more than the promises of lust can we find complete healing. Winning is an inside job and it is the power of God that makes it possible!

Peter Takes A Walk

The image of Peter walking on the water has inspired followers of Christ down through the centuries (Matthew 14:22-32). When Jesus came walking on the stormy sea, all of the Disciples were terrified and cried out in fear. Jesus told them to take courage and not be afraid. But Peter, for some unknown reason, said, "Lord, if it is you, tell me to come to you on the water." Was his motive cockiness, showing off for the other fisherman? Did he have faith that if it really were Jesus He could cause Peter to walk on

> *When your desire for Jesus is so big that it eclipses your fear of the storm, you can walk on the waters of your circumstances.*

the water, too? Whatever the motive of his heart, Peter got down out of the boat being tossed by the wind and the waves and began to walk on the water. His desire to come to Jesus was so great that it overcame his fear of the storm. He trusted in Jesus more than He trusted in the comfort and safety of the boat.

Then Peter was distracted at some point. Perhaps he walked for two or three minutes or maybe even longer. But at some point he suddenly became aware of the wind and the waves; the wind kicked up and his fears came back. When he began to sink, he cried out "Lord, save me!"

Jesus immediately reached out His hand and rescued the frightened Peter. Jesus said, "You of little faith, why did you doubt?"

How many times have you been a Peter, first trusting and then doubting that Jesus could help you overcome the storms of your sexual temptations? Some of you may have walked for many days, even years, without doubting, trusting Jesus to keep you afloat, but then something distracted you, something caused you to doubt. And once again you sank into your sexual sin.

There is a basic principle involved in this story. When your desire for Jesus is so big that it eclipses your fear of the storm, you can walk on the waters of your circumstances.

When you see Jesus bigger than the wind and waves of your sexual temptations, you can trust Him to keep you safe. When you are distracted and see the storm as more powerful than Jesus, you begin to sink. When your commitment to Jesus is the bigger "Yes!" of your life, you will be able to say "No!" to the sexual temptations that come your way.

> *Sexual distraction happens when you believe the promises of pleasure offered by lust will make you happier than the promises of Jesus.*

Sexual distraction happens when you believe that the promises of pleasure offered by lust will make you happier than trusting the promises of Jesus. The wind and waves are the promises of pleasure offered by temptations. When you believe that following Jesus and trusting His promises will make you happier than yielding to lust, you will walk in victory. Focus on the promises of God, not the waves of lust that creep into your life.

The victory that wins the battle is an inside victory. "I can do everything through Him who gives me strength." (Philippians 4:13). Where does Christ strengthen you? On the outside? Or does He give you spiritual strength on the inside?

Roots of Impurity

Jesus said that sexual immorality comes from the heart, from within the person's heart and soul (Matthew 15:18; Mark 7:20-23). The Greek word translated "immorality" is better understood to mean "impurity". Immorality in today's culture has more of a behavioral focus, but Jesus was consistent in focusing on heart motives as the root of sexual sin. Behaviors, adultery, sexual acting out or lust originate in the heart. Paul said that a man's sinful nature produced sexual immorality, impurity, debauchery and other sins (Galatians 5:19).

The Jews of Jesus' day, like many people today, made sin a set of behaviors. If a person did certain things, he had sinned. Many people felt they had not sinned because they had not done certain behaviors. But when Jesus came He said that the heart attitude was the root of the sin problem, not just the behaviors.

You have heard that it was said, 'Do not commit adultery.' but I tell you that anyone who looks at a woman lustfully has already committed adultery with her in his heart.
Matthew 5:27-28

The good man brings good things out of the good stored up in his heart, and the evil man brings evil thing out of the evil stored up in his heart. For out of the overflow of his heart his mouth speaks.
Luke 6:45

This book focuses on the root issues, not just the symptoms (the observable behaviors). God wants to heal your heart and soul where the roots of sexual impurity reside.

Sin Nature

The Scriptures teach that it is man's sin nature that is behind all of the sinful heart attitudes and sinful behaviors. Paul said that it was the sin nature in man that kept him from doing the good he desired to do (Romans 7:18). The sin nature's effect on all of your physical drives results in amplification that encourages misuse. This is true about your sexuality. Satan's strategy is to use sexual temptations to lure you into using a normal sex drive to try and satisfy emotional needs or bury your emotional pain.

Your physical drives were meant for physical purposes, not to meet your emotional needs. Your emotional needs were designed by God and are to be fulfilled through appropriate relationships and experiences. When you use a physical drive to satisfy an emotional need (i.e. food for comfort, sex for love) you are using the physical drive inappropriately. It is easy to get your life out of balance when you try to fill up empty holes in your soul through some physical drive like hunger or lust.

> *Your physical drives were meant for physical purposes, not to meet your emotional needs.*

Roots of Sinful Behaviors

All men have a sin nature and are capable of having sinful heart attitudes and sinful behaviors, but not every man commits every kind of sin. If we are honest about ourselves, we know that the possibility of every sin ever committed lies within our own hearts, and it is only by God's grace that we have not committed many of these sins. James tells us that if we commit one sin we are just as guilty as if we committed every sin (James 2:10).

> *God wants to heal your heart and soul where the roots of sexual impurity reside.*

The question then is: "Why do you commit one kind of sin, your friend commits another and others commit still different sins?" Not all men are thieves, murderers or adulterers. What causes one person to commit one kind of sin and the next guy to commit another?

I believe it is possible to understand why each person engages in different sins when you recognize the root issues in each person's life. No two people have had the same exact life experiences in their family of origin or encounters in life. These life experiences create the different nuances of each person's uniqueness.

Every person has some soul wounds and emotional pain. These wounds and pain have roots in life experiences. All people are raised in a fallen world and no one escapes without some emotional wounding and scarring. To understand the roots of your sinful behaviors, particularly your sexual difficulties, it is helpful to understand the wounds and scars you carry.

History Teaches

The Scriptures teach that your personal history is to be a teaching tool that His Spirit uses to train us and to provide us a way of teaching our children. The history of the nation Israel was to be a teaching device for God's chosen people. God enshrined the major events of their history with altars and festivals to memorialize the things. He

> *God uses history to teach His people.*

wanted them to teach their children (Exodus 12:14, 26; Joshua 4:4-7). Paul writes that the history of Israel recorded in the Old Testament is to teach you and to warn you (I Corinthians 10:1-12, Romans 15:4). God uses history to teach His people.

In a similar manner you can study your family history to gain understanding about the causes and effects of certain behaviors and events. You function much like a medical doctor who takes a medical history when a patient first comes to his office. He does this so he can understand what might be or what might not be causing the person's illness. Likewise, the Lord

> *The events of the past do not cause the sin, but they do pre-condition you to be vulnerable to certain sins.*

wants you to understand the roots of your behaviors so you can find healing for your wounds.

The purpose of looking at your childhood is not to find someone to blame, but to try and understand what the emotional wounds are which trigger your sexual issues and acting out behaviors. The events of the past do not cause the sin, but they do pre-condition you to be vulnerable to certain sins. When the wounds of abuse or unmet emotional needs connect with a normal sexual drive, the combination can lead easily into sexual urges that are out of control.

Unmet Emotional Needs and Wounds

Your unmet emotional needs and emotional wounds become unconscious drivers of your sexuality. This is a critical point to understand if you are going to win the battle and gain self-control sexually. Your wounds do not cause you to sin sexually, but often you may attempt to heal or fix your emotional wounds by using sex as a band-aid or anesthetic.

> *Your unmet emotional needs and emotional wounds become unconscious drivers of your sexuality.*

When you have an emotional need or wound, you will attempt to resolve that need or wound in some way. Even children adapt to painful environments by seeking the attention they need in ways that work. If a child cannot get love and attention by being a good child, then he/she might become the bad child. Negative attention is better than no attention. Whatever the unmet emotional need or emotional pain is, individuals try to find some way to satisfy the need or some way to alleviate the pain. When they are unable to cure the cause, they will revert to behaviors that simply deaden the pain. Much of the sexual acting-out in this culture is about avoiding or medicating the emotional pains of life.

Emotional Pain Diagram

Every person carries in his heart and soul a quantity of emotional pain. It can be diagramed this way:

Some people have a large quantity of pain in their life; some have a small amount of pain, but everyone has some.

> **Sex can make a great band-aid or anesthetic.**

Today's society teaches people directly and by example that they do not have to deal with pain ("Take two aspirin and call me tomorrow."). They avoid pain or anesthetize pain with distractions like TV, work, shopping, food or other means. They deaden pain with alcohol, drugs or sex. Whatever you use to avoid or deaden pain can become an addiction.

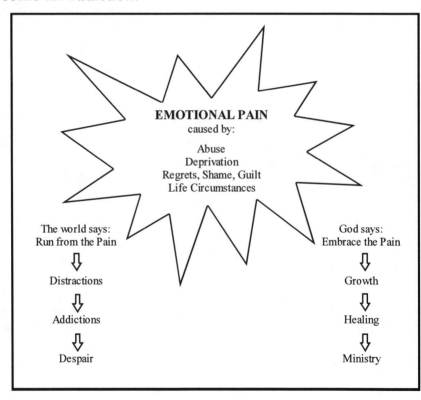

EMOTIONAL PAIN
caused by:

Abuse
Deprivation
Regrets, Shame, Guilt
Life Circumstances

The world says:
Run from the Pain
⇩
Distractions
⇩
Addictions
⇩
Despair

God says:
Embrace the Pain
⇩
Growth
⇩
Healing
⇩
Ministry

When you embrace pain instead of running from it, God promises that He will cause all these roots of your pain to work together for your growth, your healing and His glory (Romans 8:28). You must be willing to own the pain and accept it as real. God will then enable you to find healing.

Sexual behaviors, like pornography and all sorts of acting-out, are used to deaden emotional pain. Sex can be a great band-aid or anesthetic.

Infected Wounds

If a person has a wound, such as a cut on his hand, and he does not take care of that wound, it can get infected by bacteria and germs. A similar process takes place with wounds in your heart and soul.

> **Satan's power is in the lie.**

Satan infects these wounds with lies and deceptions. Satan's power is in the lie.

> *. . . there is no truth in him. When he (Satan) lies, he speaks his native language, for he is a liar and the father of lies.*
>
> John 8:44

Satan's only power over you is the power you give him by failing to take every thought captive and by being deceived by his schemes (II Corinthians 2:11). Your defense is to walk in the light of God's truth. Truth is your friend and your protection against the wiles of the devil. Dealing with Satan is not so much a power encounter as it is a truth encounter. When you expose his lies with God's truth, his power is broken. This is why Satan loves secrets (Luke 12:2-3) and why God wants to shine His light into all the dark places

> **Dealing with Satan is not so much a power encounter as it is a truth encounter.**

in the world and in our lives (Hebrews 4:13; John 1:4-5,9; I John 1:5-7).

The Battle for the Mind

The Scriptures clearly teach that the Christian life involves warfare. It is warfare in the spiritual realm. Paul writes:

> *For our struggle is not against flesh and blood, but against the rulers, against the authorities, against the powers of this dark world and against the spiritual forces of evil in the heavenly realms.*
>
> Ephesians 6:12

And the battlefield is your mind.

> *For though we live in the world, we do not wage war as the world does. The weapons we fight with are not the weapons of the world. On the contrary, they have divine power to demolish strongholds. We demolish arguments and every pretension that sets itself up against the knowledge of God, and we take captive every thought to make it obedient to Christ.*
>
> 2 Corinthians 10:3-5

The average Christian has no idea how his life has been impacted by the cultural brine we live in. Our minds have been gradually pickled by the messages of our culture, particularly in the area of sexuality. Do you remember the story that describes how to boil a frog? When you place a frog in a pot of cold water and gradually elevate the heat, the frog does not jump out because it never recognizes that the water is slowly getting hotter and hotter. That's what's happening in our world today. The cultural brine has pickled many Christians without our even realizing it.

Bondage through Soul Ties

Paul writes in I Corinthians that a sexual relationship between two partners involves deeper connections than most people want to acknowledge (I Corinthians 6:15-16). "One flesh" bonding occurs whenever partners have sexual contact, married or not. There is some kind of "soul glue" that binds the persons emotionally and spiritually.

> *The "one flesh" bonding occurs whenever partners have sexual contact, married or not.*

God designed sex to be that kind of experience. Through the hormones, exchange of bodily fluids and sharing of your soul with another person, a part of your soul and spirit gets stuck to that person. This bonding is called a "soul tie".

Remember the material about oxytocin in Chapter Five. There is a biochemical bonding that takes place as well as a spiritual and emotional bonding. Satan uses these "soul ties" to create flash-backs, to undermine trust, to encourage comparisons and to distract you from your marriage partner.

Satan is quick to use this kind of connection to keep you in deception and bondage. Through memories and through lies about yourself and relationships, Satan weaves his deceptive webs. Soul ties must be renounced and broken by the power of God.

CHAIN BREAKERS

√ Focus on the Deliverer, not the process of being delivered.

√ When your desire for God is so big it eclipses your temptations, you are able to walk in victory.

√ God wants to heal your heart and soul, not just change your behaviors.

√ You have some soul wounds and emotional pain. Ask God to show you the truth about yourself.

√ You must be willing to own the pain.

√ Remember the story about boiling the frog.

Chapter Eight

"What Motivates Humans Sexually?"

Many times what motivates you sexually is not really about sex at all. Unmet emotional needs and emotional wounds become unconscious drivers for your sexuality. A woman who engages in sex when what she really wants is affection is using sex to meet her need for emotional closeness and affection. When a man uses seduction to conquer a woman,

> *Many times what motivates you sexually is not really about sex at all.*

he is using sex to express certain emotions or feelings that may have little to do with sex. Sex wears many disguises in human relationships. Many of these masks have very little to do with a normal sex drive.

In my own battle to understand my sexual struggles, God enabled me to see the emotional drivers that empowered the sexual issues in my life. In the counseling office, God gave me insight into the emotional needs and wounds of people and the way they often used sex to meet emotional needs or to medicate emotional pain.

Normal Sex Drive

The majority of people are born with a normal sex drive, and this normal God-designed sex drive is perhaps the easiest of all biological drives to control. To illustrate, picture yourself trying to escape from a burning building. You wouldn't stop to take a look at pornography or to masturbate. Even if a gorgeous woman offered herself to you, you wouldn't indulge because the biological drive for survival is much stronger than your sex drive. You stop having sexual urges, but you keep on breathing and you keep on eating and fighting for survival when a crisis arises.

So why does your sex drive feel so hard to control?

When your normal sex drive connects with your unmet emotional needs or emotional wounds, it feels out of control. The sexual impulses feel overwhelming even though you might not be aware of any of the emotional issues amplifying your physical urges. Because these emotional drivers are functioning at an unconscious level, it's not easy to understand their role in your strong desires. Many people simply assume they have no control over their sexual urges. This is not true!

Understanding Emotional Drivers

Few people understand the role of emotional issues in their lives. As we discussed in Chapter Seven, every person has some emotional pain and develops strategies to cope with this pain. A man attempts to resolve a need or heal a wound through some behavior that he believes will work.

> *"Emotional Driver" is a term we use when we speak of an unconscious process that motivates a person.*

The behavior used to meet the emotional issue is really only a symptom of the problem the person must deal with. Too often in counseling or in ministering to these individuals, well-meaning advisors or friends address the symptoms and not the real issue. God wants to heal the emotional wounds behind the behavioral symptoms.

This process can be illustrated by what happens when a person tries to quit smoking. He may stop the behavior of smoking, but unless he addresses the emotional issues behind the smoking, he has only changed symptoms. How many smokers gain 20 pounds after they quit smoking? They stopped the behavior, but did not deal with the emotional issue. This is a major reason many people fail to break bad habits. They simply replace one bad habit with

some less offensive bad habit. The same process works in dieting. You can control your intake
of food, but if you don't heal the emotional reasons behind the over-eating, a diet will never be successful.

Emotional drivers is the term we use when we speak of the unconscious processes that motivate every person. We all have areas of unmet emotional needs or emotional wounds, and these issues influence the choices we make and the habits we develop. Until we allow God to show us these unconscious issues we cannot find healing. Emotional wounds can be healed by God, but first they must become real to you. When you own the reality of their existence, God's healing power can be focused on these issues.

But there is another reason cognitive choices don't work. They often don't address the real issues and they stir up even deeper factors.

The Feeling of Failure

Below is a composite of words I have heard so many times in counseling. For many of you these feelings and words may be all too familiar:

"I'm alone now with my thoughts and all the self-condemnation. You know the 'after.' Even when I know Jesus is here, I feel like I can only repent and ask for forgiveness and make promises to myself and God that I won't do it again. I hang my head in shame, fully aware of the knowledge that I knew exactly what I was doing. There is no excuse. No one misled me. I was wrong.

Tonight was just a bad night. I came home late and I was tired. I wanted to be productive and get things done and not waste anymore time tonight. Sexual addiction is so humiliating to me. It makes no sense. Before I know what I'm doing, I'm into it. I know I ought to stop, but the adrenaline is flowing. I am aroused.

I think I can stop, but I keep going.
After, there is only guilt and remorse. I have wasted two or three hours and lots of money on porn sites again. At least I didn't involve anyone else in this episode. And then you wake up in the morning with the memory of the night before and there is no way to erase it. It is real.

The time was wasted. The money is gone and now you have to face all your Christian friends. You hear that voice in your head: 'You're such a fraud! What if they find out about your secret? Would they want to hang around with a sex addict like you?'

And as the day goes on, you beat yourself up and promise that you will never do it again. But a few days later the memory is gone and you find yourself right back there again."

The cycle repeats itself over and over again. It sure sounds like what Paul wrote about in the seventh chapter of Romans!

So I find this law at work: when I want to do good evil is right there with me. For in my inner being, I delight in God's law, but I see another law at work in the members of my body, waging war against the law of my mind and making me a prisoner of the law of sin at work within my members. What a wretched man I am! Who will rescue me from this body of death?

Romans 7:21-24

When God transformed your heart at the moment of salvation, He took out "a heart of stone" and replaced it with a "heart of flesh" (Ezekiel 36:26-27). The old heart of stone was cold, hard, unfeeling. The new heart of flesh is alive, warm, loving and feeling. For you and me as Believers, even when we have let sin dominate, there are vibrations inside of that new heart.

It is the new heart that calls us back to the Father over and over again. The Holy Spirit, living in us, is the energy of the new heart, and He keeps guiding us, with God's power and love, back to purity. That's why Paul could write:

Therefore, there is now no condemnation for those who are in Christ Jesus.

Romans 8:1

Why Resolutions Don't Work

Most Christians, when they first feel out of control, establish resolutions or rules to help maintain control. You make rules about what you will not do and what you will do. "I will not masturbate anymore." "I will not look at porn." "I will be celibate until I marry." These are good rules! But the sin nature reacts to any rule (law) with rebellion. Paul says the law principle activates the sin nature:

> The sin nature reacts to any rule (law) with rebellion.

But sin, seizing the opportunity afforded by the commandment, produced in me every kind of covetous desire. For apart from law, sin is dead.

Romans 7:8

He says in Romans 5:20 that the law was given so that sin might increase, and in Galatians 3:24 that the law is designed to convince you of your need for Christ.

The more rules you make, the bigger the struggle. So you make promises to yourself, maybe to God. When you fail to maintain control, the guilt and shame increase and your desperation grows. A cycle of trying, failing, feeling guilty and ashamed, is followed by new resolutions and trying, followed by failing. The cycle tends to repeat itself over and over again.

Your sin nature reacts to any rule or law, increasing the temptation and the urge to rebel. So something that appears good actually stirs your sexual urges even more. Rules, "oughts" and "shoulds" become the law that your sin nature rebels against. The sin nature's reaction to your promises and desperation in not being able to maintain control leads you into even deeper guilt and shame.

Purity Is Not Perfection!

There is confusion in some Christian groups about the word "perfect".

Be perfect, therefore, as your heavenly Father is perfect.
Matthew 5:48

The word "perfect" in this passage and the way it is used in the New Testament is not speaking of sinless perfection as some Christians often preach. Throughout the New Testament and in early Greek usage the word translated "perfect" means full-growth, maturity, completeness. In the Christian sense it means full maturity in the Spirit and is contrasted in several passages with immaturity (Hebrews 5:13-14; I Corinthians 2:6-3:1).

Satan has used this word to beat us down, and it has been preached as a tool to sabotage many believers. In our Christian culture the word "perfect" has been defined "being entirely without fault or defect" even though dictionaries offer other definitions. So in frustration, many Christians respond, "Well, since I can't be perfect, why bother to try?" And Satan cheers from his grandstand seat!

A Combination of Factors

When you combine the pickling power of today's culture with your despair, it is easy to begin rationalizing about failure. One individual said, *"To rationalize is to tell yourself rational lies."*

Today's culture lures you with multiple tempting images and possibilities every hour of every day through suggestive advertising, media images and individuals who have surrendered to their passions. It is a struggle for anyone to have success in maintaining self-control. When you combine your reaction to law and rules with the pickling power of our culture, you have a serious problem. It is no wonder that many men have struggles with sex and self-control.

> When the emotional needs and wounds that hook up with your sex drive have been identified, you can bring them before the Lord and allow Him to heal these issues.

Remember, winning the battle is an inside job. In order to win the battle the issues that amplify your sexual urges must be identified and faced. Most of these issues have emotional needs and wounds as a major component of the drivers. When the emotional needs and wounds that hook up with your sex drive have been identified, you can bring them before the Lord and allow Him to heal those issues.

However, there is a factor that complicates this process of identifying unconscious drivers: most people live life on an unconscious level. You just get up in the morning and let the daily forces of life take you wherever these forces may go without your giving much thought to the whole process. It's like you are floating on a fast flowing river, letting the river take you wherever it wants to go.

Until you decide to live life consciously and begin to

look at yourself and why you do what you do, you will be at the mercy of your unconscious drivers. I encourage individuals to ask God to help them understand what is-sues He wants them to see in their unconscious. I suggest that they make Psalm 139:23-24 their personal prayer and open their hearts to what He wants them to understand.

Identifying What Motivates You

C. S. Lewis wrote that our sinful lusts are really mis-placed attempts to answer deeper needs. What motivates us sexually is from these deeper needs. There are many emotional issues and emotional wounds that can stimulate sexual urges. In some situations, more than one emo-tional issue can be involved. Ask God to give you an un-derstanding of what your emotional drivers are and allow your A&E Partners (see Chapter Fourteen) to assist you as well. There are five major emotional issues that activate and stimulate normal sex feelings and give you the sensa-tion that your sexual urges are out of control.

(1) Hunger for Affection & Un-differentiated Love Feelings:

Your skin is the largest sensory organ on your body. Ev-ery child needs lots of affection and touch to develop in a normal and healthy manner. Research is confirming that touch deprivation can be a factor in learning difficulties, anger and inability to feel empathy. Research shows that children who are not touched often struggle with intimacy and trust issues. Children who are deprived of touch and affection from their parents often grow up with a hunger for affection and touch. While the need is for non-erotic affection and touch, these individuals often use sex to try to meet these needs. (We discussed un-differentiated love feelings in Chapter Four.)

Stan grew up in an non-affectionate home. He has no memories of his mother or father being affectionate with him or his siblings, and he can barely remember a time he ever saw his parents being affectionate with one another. The only touching he remembers is being spanked by his father.

Because there was little or no affection, Stan was unable to differentiate his love feelings. All affection had erotic overtones and he had a significant hunger for affection. His biggest sexual fantasy focused on some female wanting to be with him. Stan felt he could never get enough affection, so he was always hugging everyone.

Stan's sexual feelings were stimulated by his hunger for affection and his un-differentiated love feelings.

(2) **Affirmation of Masculine Identity:**

"An automatic and serious consequence of man's failure to be affirmed is that he will suffer from low self-esteem."
Leann Payne

The masculine personality is shaped by God's design and by the flow of hormones through the male's body. But a man's sense of worth as a man is shaped in and through the interactions he does or does not have with his parents.

Since masculinity is bestowed, literally absorbed by the boy, during interaction with his father or other older males, a boy's relationship with his father is critical. If the young male does not receive affirmation of his masculinity from his father or father surrogates, he often struggles to prove to himself that he is a real man. This struggle can continue his entire life.

> A woman can never bestow masculinity on a boy.

When a young boy has experienced father-deprivation he often lacks confidence in his masculine identity. These un-affirmed males look for one or more ways to boost their masculine confidence. They are not sure they are "real men" and they set out to prove to themselves they really are.

"This is every man's deepest fear: to be exposed, to be found out, to be discovered as an imposter and not really a man."
John Eldredge, *Wild at Heart*

Sexual conquests, whether real or imagined with fantasy and masturbation, are often used to confirm they are real men. Often the thrill of the conquest is mixed with a hunger for words of affirmation, some response from the woman to affirm or reassure the boy inside that he is now a man. Un-affirmed males are seeking masculine validation, but they are seeking it from females. A woman can never bestow masculinity on a boy. She can either respond to his masculinity or she can emasculate him. Mothers, girlfriends and wives cannot bestow masculinity. They may respond to what they sense in the male, but they cannot give what they do not possess themselves.

Un-affirmed young males are often targets for predators, both homosexual and heterosexual.

Chip, a big handsome guy in his late twenties, confirmed with tears running down his face, that he never felt delighted in by a man until he gave a man sexual pleasure. Chip's dad had died when he was three years old and he was reared by a single mom. Since there was no father present, he never received the affirmation and love he needed from a man.

Women need to understand that most men they know have two big emotional and relational issues. The first issue is the one we just discussed, the man's need to have his masculinity affirmed. The second issue involves the fear of intimacy.

(3) **Fear of Intimacy:**

When a boy is raised in a home where his father is absent, passive, or just not present emotionally, his mother can have too much emotional input and control over the boy's life. To compound the problem, some mothers can be controlling, overly emotional or manipulative. By the time an average young male is ten to twelve years of age he has had all of the mothering he wants. If, for whatever reason, the mother is intrusive,

> Some men use sex as a way to keep women at a distance.

smothering, controlling or just overly involved in the boy's life, he develops ways to keep women at a distance emotionally. These males have an unconscious driver that says, *"I will never let another women have that kind of control over me again."* If a man turns a woman into a sex object, he thinks he knows what to do with her and it certainly does not involve having to connect emotionally. *"There is no way she will control me!"*

Men often tease other men who allow their wives to have too much control. They call them "hen-pecked" and other derogatory names. Nothing embarrasses or stirs an un-affirmed man's anger like having another guy accuse him of what he fears.

If a woman is seen as a sex object, he knows how to deal with her. There are other ways men keep women at a distance emotionally and relationally; we are just addressing the sexual issues in this book.

(4) **Abandonment Issues:**

Many men will seek sexual gratification as a means of dealing with loneliness, hunger for companionship or a desire for some emotional connection. These men often experienced emotional and physical abandonment in childhood or at some time in their adult lives.

Brad was raised in an orphanage. He only experienced painful, shallow or abusive relationships. He learned, at an early age, that some people would connect with him sexually, so sex became his primary way to connect with people.

Many men have confessed in counseling that the only time they ever felt connected to another person was through sex. Some of these men talked about early homosexual experiences, but many reported sexual activities with older women.

Don told about his fifth grade teacher having sex with him. Eric bragged about having an affair with a thirty-two year old woman when he was eight years old. Unfortunately, in our culture, there is a tragic disparity: a young girl is abused, a young boy "gets lucky".

Make no mistake about it.
Both are examples of sexual abuse!

Many men do not understand the role of emotions and feelings in relationships, so their ability to connect in non-sexual ways is limited. Sex becomes a tool to make them feel connected. It makes a good anesthetic for abandonment and loneliness. One man put it this way, "Hey, anything is better than isolation and abandonment!"

(5) **Anger and Hostility:**

> Anger is often a significant factor in sexual motivation.

Most people do not think about anger as a factor in sexual motivation, but it may be one of the most significant in today's culture. Rape is obviously more about anger than it is about sex. But there are other ways that men and women can express anger through sexual issues. Adultery always has an anger component toward the spouse. Seduction can have a strong anger component: *"If I seduce you, I have conquered you."* Objectifying a woman is also an expression of anger; the other person is simply seen as body parts to be used for pleasure. A man fantasizing about another woman while he is having sex with his wife could be seen as anger and emotional rejection. Sexual comments, undressing a woman with your eyes, calling a woman sexual terms and withholding sex in your marriage are some other ways anger and sex mingle in men's lives. Many of the sexual activities in today's culture have anger and hostility components associated with them. The role of anger in intimate relationships is a topic worthy of much more discussion than what we can do in this book.

Additional Factors

While the five emotional issues listed above are the major ones that can stimulate sexual urges, there are other factors, observed in my life
and in the lives of the people I have counseled, that empower these urges. Here is a brief discussion of five of them.

(1) *Repressed Curiosity:*
Every child has a normal curiosity about the opposite sex. When there is a brother or sister in the house, it is very normal for young children (ages 4 to 7) to play doctor or some other *"I'll show you mine if you show me yours"* kind of game. When parents distract children to play other games, the children soon forget their curious interest. But when parents freak out and use guilt and shame to shut down a child's curiosity, it is often repressed only to resurface in teen or young adult years.

Robert remembers his normal curiosity about the opposite sex as a very shameful thing; innocent questions were met with harsh disapproval by his parents. At the same time, he had a young aunt living in his home who had a habit of leaving the bathroom door open when she was dressing, giving Robert an uncensored and ongoing view of her feminine form. There was something "thrilling" about nudity. As a grown married man, he secretly took some nude massage classes and visited a nudist group. A woman sharing herself through nudity made him feel very special. "I must be important to her for her to let me see. If she gives herself to me visually and sexually, she must love me."

(2) *Sexual Wounds*:

When a boy is abused or sexualized in childhood, the images, guilt and shame feed into sexual activities later in life. When a young male is exposed to adult nudity or adult sexual activities which can stimulate him beyond what is appropriate for his age, it can become a serious empowering issue in his unconscious. Re-enactment of early sexualizing life situations or sexual trauma has great emotional energy for many men. Exposure to nudity or pornography stimulates and energizes a young male's sexual urges. Robert, from the previous story, reported that for many years he could close his eyes and see his aunt standing in the bathroom naked. The experience fueled his desires to look at pornography and topless dancers.

All addictions can be fatal if not addressed.

(3) *Sexual Addiction*:

In the addictive process, all of the unconscious emotional drivers can be utilized to stir a man's sexual activities as well as his use of sex to bury, medicate, anesthetize, or avoid the emotional pain in his life. (See the Emotional Pain Diagram in Chapter Seven.) A person can become addicted to any substance (alcohol, drugs, food) or activity (sex, work, sports) that he uses to keep from feeling his emotional pain.

In sexual addiction, like all other addictions, the addict eventually becomes absorbed with the sexual activities, the pursuit, the acting out. It progresses until it controls his life and eventually will lead to high risk or illegal behaviors. All addictions can be fatal if not addressed.

(4) *Sexualized Habits:*

Sexual habits are a factor with sex addicts, but they can also impact other men who feel they have no addiction problem. Pornography, masturbation, voyeurism, uncontrolled imagination and appetites all become habitual. The adrenaline and other hormones that are released with the pursuit of sexual activities are addicting and reinforce the habits. Many counselors argue that these individuals are simply in denial about the addictive process.

(5) *Hunger for Pleasure:*

Lasciviousness is the term used in the Scriptures for this insatiable appetite. Men who have given themselves over to sexual and other "physical pleasures" become self-centered, self-absorbed, greedy, and covetous. They have given themselves over to their appetites and once the lasciviousness and sensuality have taken hold, their hunger for pleasure drives them sexually. Satan hooks up with the person's sin nature to encourage the pursuit of pleasure.

All of the items listed above can have intense emotional energy involved. When that need or that wound connects with the normal sex drive, it magnifies and energizes your sexual impulses.

> *Any time a normal biological drive is used to meet non-biological needs, it can become an unhealthy situation.*

Any time a normal biological drive is used to meet non-biological needs, it can become an unhealthy situation. This is what

113

happens with many people struggling with weight problems. They are eating for emotional reasons, not body needs. Food is to be used as fuel and not for comfort or to bury emotional pain. The human sex drive was designed to meet the relational and procreation needs in the marriage relationship. When it connects with unmet emotional needs, it becomes an unhealthy driving force.

We've listed five major emotional issues that activate and stimulate normal sex feelings and give you the sensation that your sexual urges are out of control:

(1) Hunger for Affection and Un-differentiated Love Feelings

(2) Affirmation of Masculine Identity

(3) Fear of Intimacy

(4) Abandonment Issues

(5) Anger and Hostility

We then listed five additional factors:

(1) Repressed Curiosity

(2) Sexual Wounds

(3) Sexual Addictions

(4) Sexualized Habits

(5) Hunger for Pleasure

The normal human sex drive was designed by God

to be under the control of the individual's volition (will). When emotional wounds or unmet emotional needs link up with the sex drive, people often feel their sexual urges are so powerful they cannot control them. When these wounds, needs and other factors are identified and isolated from the sex drive, the individual can find healing. God can help you discover ways to meet your emotional needs in a healthy manner and He can provide healing for all of the factors listed.

A Personal Strategy for Healing

Paul says that we are to break out of the mold of this world:

Do not conform any longer to the pattern of this world, but be transformed by the renewing of your mind.

Romans 12:2

Ask God to reprogram your mind. Then intentionally expose yourself to His truth over and over again. The Scriptures are used by the Holy Spirit to transform our minds and to heal our memories, but you must be an intentional warrior.

> **Ask God to reprogram your mind.**

You do not casually overcome the strongholds of the enemy. Ask the Holy Spirit to make you aware of every area where you have been impacted by the cultural brine and the personal lies of Satan. Trust the Holy Spirit to enable you to demolish each and every stronghold.

Each day put on the full armor of God (Ephesians 6:10-18) and walk in the light as Jesus is in the light. The Holy Spirit will guide you into all truth (John 16:13) and He will empower you to win the internal battle. In this manner, you will each day put to death whatever belongs to your earthly nature (Colossians 3:5).

Freedom from Unconscious Drivers

Unhealed memories account for many of the unconscious drivers that motivate us sexually. Freedom from emotional issues that drive our sexual urges is a critical part of our ability to maintain sexual purity. Gaining control and healing these drivers must be a priority. Understanding provides confidence and a sense of control for most people.

> *In this book, you are learning a new software package that gives you knowledge and understanding about your sexual feelings and how to control them.*

When you understand how a piece of equipment or software works, you have a sense of power and control over that equipment or software. To illustrate this idea, picture arriving at the office where you work only to find a new software package on your computer. It is software you are not familiar with and have no working knowledge of, so you have no power or sense of control over the computer. But once you learn the software, you have the ability to make it work for you.

Your sexuality works the same way. What you have been learning in this book is like a new software package that gives you new knowledge and understanding about your sexual feelings and how you can control them. The next step is to provide you with some practical "how to" training.

Specific Steps to Address
Issues of Unconscious Drivers

• <u>Commit Yourself to live by God's Purposes for Sex.</u>

Choose to live by God's purposes and design within His boundaries, not by your urges. As long as you resent God's plan, purposes and boundaries, you will have difficulty living according to them. Accept by faith God's instructions as being the best way to live your life. This commitment will need to be affirmed daily as you work to break the power of the unconscious issues and factors in your life.

• Pray Psalm 139:23-24.

Search me, O God, and know my heart; test me and know my anxious thoughts. See if there is any offensive way in me, and lead me in the way everlasting.

Ask God to show you what the issues and factors are that have linked together with your normal sex drive to cause you to feel out of control.

• <u>Ask God to Meet Your Emotional Needs and Heal Your Emotional Wounds.</u>

Reject the ungodly, unhealthy ways you have used to meet your needs. Expect God to show you how He can meet your needs in a healthy way and how He will bring healing for your emotional wounds.

• <u>Offer Your Body to God as an Instrument for His Purposes</u>

Do not offer the parts of your body to sin, as instruments of wick-
edness, but rather offer yourselves to God . . . and offer the parts of
your body to Him as instruments of righteousness.

Romans 6:13

God had a purpose in mind when He created you.
Commit yourself and your body to fulfill the purpose for
which He created you.

For we are God's workmanship, created in Christ Jesus to do good
works which God prepared in advance for us to do.

Ephesians 2:10

- <u>Break Your Connection to the World's View of Sex.</u>

Deliberately choose to get out of the brine and reprogram your mind with God's truth (Romans 12:1-2). Once
you have yielded to your sensuality, it is difficult to bring
it back under control, but God can help you. Once you
commit to His Lordship and sincerely desire His will for
your life, the Holy Spirit will help you make the difficult
choices.

- <u>Learn to See People as Jesus Does.</u>

People are not just bodies to be used. They are souls
wrapped in skin. They are individual souls that will live for
eternity. They are persons with great worth to God and
Jesus died for each and every one of them. Accept and
honor the differences without sexualizing the differences.

CHAIN BREAKERS

√ What motivates you sexually is often more than your normal sex drive. Self-control is about consciously disconnecting the sex drive from your emotional wounds and needs.

√ God has put a new heart in you. Allow the Holy Spirit to empower your new heart to defeat the lusts of the flesh.

√ Choose to change your life. It is a matter of your will, submitted to the Holy Spirit, not rules and regulations.

√ Ask God to show you what your emotional drivers are. Pray for His healing touch on each of these drivers (Psalm 139:23-24).

√ Reaffirm your commitment to God's purposes, His design and His desires for your sexuality.

Chapter Nine

"Getting a Grip on Temptation"

Temptation is not a battle lost. Temptation is the normal plight of Christians. Ninety percent of all Christian men face lust and sexual temptations. Temptations are common to man (I Corinthians 10:13). They are evidence of life and the desire you have to live in spiritual purity. If that desire were not there, there would be no temptations.

The mistake we make is that we focus on external temptations not internal causes. The emotional needs or wounds a person has on the inside determine what he is tempted by on the outside. Temptations are Satan's attempt to sow seed in your heart and soul. Temptation finds fertile soil when there are certain emotional issues that have prepared the soil of your soul to receive an evil seed.

In temptation, Satan is not really tempting you to do bad things, he is tempting you toward spiritual infidelity. He is challenging your trust in God. He wants to cause you to lose what God has been building into you...the possibility of being of value to God. So he raises questions about your identity

> *The emotional needs or wounds a person has on the inside determine what he is tempted by on the outside.*

as a man, about God's character and ability, and he even causes you to question God's desires to take care of you. Temptation does not start with a visual image. It starts with the question: "Did God really say...?"

Satan changes the question he asked Eve in the Garden (Genesis 3:1) to a similar question when he comes to tempt you: "Did God really say you are not to enjoy sex outside of marriage?" And the challenge to Eve is the same challenge that Satan makes to you: "You will not surely die..."

(Genesis 3:4). The implication Satan makes to Christians every day through sexual temptations is that God is withholding something from us. Satan wants us to question the character of God and His loving desire to provide for His people.

Satan's lies never change. They always call God's character into question. As a Christian you have to choose to either trust the character of God revealed through Jesus Christ or the lies Satan repeats with every sexual temptation. Satan is the god of the cultural brine, and one of the ways he works is to steal your imagination.

Stolen Imagination

Imagination is a wonderful gift that God gave to mankind. With the imagination, you plan, you set goals, you remember special events; you visualize and set goals for the future. Your imagination lives outside of time and can be used to remember the past, picture the future or to enrich the present. Your imagination is similar to a built in DVD player. Your brain replays events, remembers the feelings and evaluates the outcomes.

> Satan has stolen the gift of imagination from the average Christian.

Oswald Chambers wrote, "Imagination is the greatest gift God has given us and it ought to be devoted entirely to Him." Imagination is the mental faculty that is essential to creativity and, like most of God's gifts, it should be sanctified and used to bring honor and glory to God. It is a wonderful gift from God.

But remember that Satan came to steal, kill and destroy (John10:10) and your imagination is one of his primary targets.

Satan steals your imagination so it does not enrich your life. You cannot remember the joy of the past; you cannot anticipate the joy of the future and you cannot utilize it to enrich your daily spiritual life. Here is how the enemy of your soul does this damaging deed:

Satan steals your past with regrets.

This involves the "if onlys" of your life. "If only I hadn't done this or that." Your imagination concerning your past history is captured and used to bring to your mind all of the regrets you have about your mistakes, your moral failures, your shame and guilt. He robs you of your joyful memories and hinders your ability to learn from your history. He also uses shame and guilt to paralyze you and keep you from stepping out in ministry opportunities.

I believe it is this guilt and shame that paralyzes many Christians and that it is a major reason why the average church congregation is filled with more spectators than participators. God wants Christians to stop watching and waiting. He wants us to be initiators and impact our world!

Satan steals your future with fears.

This involves the "what ifs" of your life. "What if this or that happens in the future?" Your imagination concerning your future and the possibilities for tomorrow is stained with all sorts of fears. In this way Satan robs you of your joy about the future and paralyzes your creativity. Your fears hinder you from visualizing what God wants to accomplish through you.

Satan steals your present with lust.

The imagination that you can use for prayer and ministry is captured and used for lustful fantasies. This is the way Satan steals your time, money and boldness for ministry. He will use it to destroy your family and all of your relationships. Your secrets become unexploded bombs that he can bring to mind at any time in any place.

The Power of the Imagination

The power of the imagination lies in the fact that the human mind does not distinguish between vividly imagined experiences and real life experiences. Professional golfers and other athletes use this concept to program their minds and bodies for higher levels of performance in competition. Golfers pre-play a golf shot or even an entire round of golf, visualizing each shot. Great athletes visualize an entire game or race in their imagination many times before they actually play the game or run the race. The electronic pathways in their brains are programmed for maximum concentration and performance.

Your imagination works the same way with your sexual experiences. When you have a sexual encounter, your mind and body interact and release the hormones that make sex pleasurable. It happens the way God designed the body to work. In a similar manner, when you vividly fantasize about a sexual experience, your mind and body interact in the same way and release the same hormones to bring sexual pleasure. Most people know the power of sexual fantasies. Instead of using their imagination for God's glory, many Christians use it to carry them into the deeper realms of sinful sensuality.

Imagination and Temptation

Remember the scene from Chevy Chase's "National Lampoon's Vacation" movie, where an attractive woman passes him while all the family is asleep? We all laughed because we had been there or some place similar. Some simple stimulation and the imagination takes off. We drift along letting our imagination create all kinds of scenarios. Some of us lived through our imagination for much of our young adult life.

> *We need to learn to control our imagination more than our eyes.*

The issue is not the stimulus, what we see, the real issue is our untrained, undisciplined imagination. It is not what we see, but what we allow our imagination to do with what we see. We need to learn to control our imagination more than our eyes. In Chapter Eleven, we introduce a strategy called CPR for Lust. It refocuses our imaginations so that they become instruments of righteousness instead of our own personal "internet style" porn factories.

> *The issue is not what you see, but what your imagination does with what you think you see.*

As you train your imagination, it becomes like a Teflon coated pan, nothing immoral sticks.

Remember the issue is not what you see, but what your imagination does with what you think you see. There are millions of stimulating, impulse generating things we will encounter throughout our lives. The key is to reign in your imagination and develop Teflon style of thinking. The impulses may come, but they don't stick because the imagination is coated with spiritual Teflon.

Pathways in the Brain

Scientific research has discovered that your thoughts create neural pathways in your brain when you think the same thoughts over and over again. It is similar to what happens when you walk across your lawn day after day. Your repetitious walk, along the same path, begins to wear a pathway across the grass. After a period of time, the path becomes a rut and the grass has disappeared. The deeper the path, the harder it is to walk a different path and blaze a new

> *When Satan steals your imagination, he is programming your mind to think the same thoughts over and over again.*

trail. This is one of the reasons habits are hard to break.

When you engage in repeated sexual fantasies, you are creating neural pathways through your brain. After many years of these fantasies, you have established well-worn pathways and habits that are very difficult to change.

When Satan steals your imagination, he is programming you to think the same thoughts over and over again. After a while, you automatically think the same thoughts in the same situation. Habits are formed and your options are limited. Satan has a chain around your heart and soul. This is one of Satan's schemes to derail you through your temptations.

Reticular Activating System

In your brain there is a critical network of cells connected to your brain stem. It is known as the reticular activating system. In a very real sense, this part of your brain acts like a gate-keeper responsible for controlling all incoming data to your mind. (from The Encyclopedia of Psychology. Edited by Rom Harre and Roger Lamb.) Stimuli from all of your senses must pass through the reticular activating system and nothing gets through the gate without permission. This system is what controls your ability to make or break habits.

The reticular activating system is the system in your brain where you program your brain to pay attention to what is important to you and what is not important to you. We have all experienced this system at work. For example, my wife and I decided that we were going to buy a new car and we settled on a red Hyunda Elantra. In the days before we made the decision we rarely, if ever, saw a red Hyunda on the streets, but the very day we made our purchase, we were shocked at the

> *The truth is you don't break a habit; you simply replace it.*

number of red Hyundas. Red Hyundas were everywhere. Since red Hyundas had become important to us, our reticular activating systems were now calling our attention to the red Hyundas everywhere. The reticular activating system was programmed by what we focused our attention on. We had programmed it to notice red Hyundas. Denis Waitley writes in Seeds of Greatness, "The reticular activating system filters out the unimportant stimuli and focuses on what is important at the moment."

The same thing happens with lust issues. When you focus your attention on shapely females, you begin to notice them everywhere. You have programmed your reticular activating system to pick up on and open the gate to sexual stimuli that spurs you toward lust issues. In order to win the battle over lust, you must reset the priorities in your own brain. By focusing your attention on spiritual truth and A&E Partnerships instead of attractive females, you begin to reprogram your reticular activating system.

> *Your brain can help you win the battle over temptation.*

The truth is you don't break a habit; you simply replace it. You have been focusing your mind on sexual stimuli and so you keep being frustrated with temptations. When you reset your priorities and reprogram your mind, your brain becomes your ally and enables you to win the battle over temptation.

The good news is that God can set you free from the chains that bind you! In fact the scientific research indicates that you can even reprogram the neural pathways in your brain. When you choose to think new thoughts and set new patterns in place in your mind, the brain begins to adjust to new neural pathways. It works in a similar way to what happens when you change the path you take across your front yard. Once you begin to walk a new path, the grass begins to grow and cover the original pathway. When you change the way you think, new neural pathways are formed in the brain and, with time and disuse, the old neural pathways disappear.

> *"What the researchers discovered not only confirmed that our [mental] programs are physical pathways in the brain; they proved we could do something about it. They learned that if a person could somehow stop using an old program long enough, the old program would actually break down chemically – all by itself! And the change is physical in the brain, measurable with sophisticated medical imaging computers."*
> Dr. Shad Helmstetter, *The Self-Talk Solution*

The Scriptures say, "Be transformed by the renewing of your mind" (Romans 12:2). When you begin the transformation process and stop being conformed to the patterns of this world, the Spirit of God enables you to grow and break patterns of your old life (I Corinthians 6:9-11).

Scientific research has discovered that to change a habit, it takes 21 days. Others say that you can change any thought pattern within 90 days. The Scriptures point to 40 days as a good number of days to allow God to do His transforming work. With God all things are possible (Luke 1:37) when you intentionally participate in His designed processes for transformation.

The importance of your brain in sexual experience is discussed in detail in Douglas Weiss's book Sex, Men and God. He writes how through "classical conditioning" our brains attach us to specific sexual images, creating pathways that influence our sexual behaviors. For those who want more information on this topic, I would recommend Weiss's excellent material. He positively states, "The good news is that you can retrain your brain for sexual success."

The Process of Temptation

The Scriptures present the process that takes place when you face temptation.

> *When tempted, no one should say, "God is tempting me." For God cannot be tempted by evil, nor does He tempt anyone; but each one is tempted when, by his own evil desire, he is dragged away and enticed. Then, after desire has conceived, it gives birth to sin; and sin, when it is full-grown, gives birth to death."*
>
> James 1:13-15

The process can be diagrammed as follows:

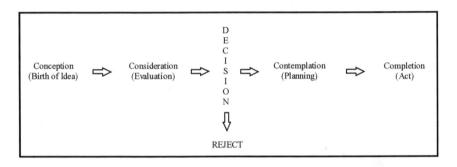

In the diagram you see the flow of the temptation process. A thought is conceived in your brain. We should never be surprised about any thought that occurs to us because our deceitful hearts, our sin nature and the suggestions (fiery darts?) of Satan can breed all kinds of evil thoughts.

Once the thought or idea is conceived, you go through the process of considering the idea or thought as to its value or worth in your life.

> *Joseph met the temptation and did not sin; David met the temptation and sinned.*

When you make a decision and reject the thought at that point of consideration, you have successfully dealt with the temptation. No sin is involved.

As you mature in your faith, you instantly recognize most issues as worthy or unworthy of consideration. The decision is made almost without effort.

The process can be illustrated with the temptation to lust. An attractive person passes by. Your brain or hormones plant the thought: "Wow! She is good looking!" You consider what you will do with that thought. You evaluate it and reject it. You have defeated the temptation to lust. No sin involved.

You can see this process illustrated clearly in the case of Joseph and the temptation by Potiphar's wife (Genesis 39). The idea or thought is planted (verse 7). Joseph quickly evaluates the offer (verses 8-9) and rejects the offer (verses 9, 12). Joseph met the temptation and did not sin.

For another illustration on the process of temptation, consider King David's experience recorded in II Samuel 11. David faced temptation with Bathsheba. His unconscious drivers were working in David when he decided to walk on the roof of his house. He was not where he was supposed to be, in the field with his army (v. 1), and he was likely feeling somewhat bored.

As he walked on his roof that spring evening he saw Bathsheba and a thought (idea) was conceived (v.2). He considers the idea. Verse 3 says: "The woman was very beautiful and David sent someone to find out about her." He learned she was the wife of one of his soldiers who was off on the battlefield with the King's army. David had moved into the contemplation (planning) stage. The next step was to have Bathsheba brought to him (completion). The stages of temptation can be easily traced through David's failure. All he needed to do to stop the process was to get off the roof! David was tempted and he sinned.

Get off the roof!

The same process can be illustrated by the three temptations of Christ in the wilderness in Luke 4. The first temptation was to turn stones to bread. Satan planted the idea, Jesus instantly evaluated and rejected it by quoting a passage of Scripture. Satan then made an appeal to power. Likewise, Jesus rejected the idea. Finally Satan made an appeal to pride; once again Jesus instantly evaluated and rejected the idea. In all three offers, Jesus rejected Satan's suggestions. Jesus was tempted, but He did not sin.

> **Jesus was tempted, but He did not sin.**

These examples from Scripture can be used as a model for facing your own temptations. As you mature in your Christian faith, this evaluation process becomes faster and requires less internal debate.

From Temptation to Sin

You should carefully evaluate every thought or idea that comes to mind in light of Scriptures and base your evaluation on the Word of God. If you decide to reject a thought or idea as unworthy, you have won the battle over temptation. If you allow the process to move to the third stage, contemplation, then you are beginning to make plans about how to act on that idea or thought. When you move past the decision line into the planning process, you move into sin.

Let's look again at the example of seeing the attractive person. You thought, "Wow! She is good looking!" That idea was the conception stage of the process, but it was not sin. You then moved into the evaluation stage. Previously, in the example, you rejected the idea and did not give it further thought. You defeated the temptation to lust. No sin was involved. But what if you had allowed your mind to continue: "She really has a great body. Wonder what it would be like to …". You made the decision to move into the contemplation stage (which is the sin of lust) and the odds increase that you will choose to move into the completion stage (which may mean self-gratification or acting-out sexually with another person). Satan has won this particular battle. You have moved from temptation (which is not a sin) into acting on the temptation which is sin.

It does not take much energy to move past the contemplation stage into the completion of the idea or thought. Sinful behavior is the end result of the process. Once you move past the decision point into the contemplation stage, the only solution for the sin is repentance and confession (I John 1:9). Repentance is turning from the sin; confession literally means to agree with God concerning your sin and His provision for the sin. There is no place for self-condemnation since the blood of Jesus has cleansed you from your sin (Romans 8:1).

> *It is always easier to properly handle temptation than it is to recover from sin and its consequences.*

An important note to remember is this: the process of handling temptation, while it may be difficult at the time, is always easier than the process of recovering from sin and its consequences. Consider what sin cost David, then consider that Joseph avoided disastrous personal consequences by not yielding to the temptation. Joseph's success at defeating temptation was costly, but he did not suffer from the consequences of sin like David did. It is always easier to properly handle temptation than it is to recover from sin and its consequences.

It is also helpful to remember that temptations do not invade our minds as easily when we are focused on important tasks. When we have downtime and our minds are in neutral, we have to be on guard.

Idle Minds

I don't know who first coined the phrase, but I can remember my Mother quoting it to me on several occasions: "An idle mind is the devil's workshop!" Most men will admit that it is when their minds are idle, not engaged in productive, exciting activities, that they are most vulnerable to serious sexual temptations.

Men who travel and work in other cities, away from friends and family, find their idle evening hours the most difficult. Alone in a hotel room with the TV or Internet, with nothing to do, these men with idle hours and unoccupied minds are vulnerable to all kinds of intrusive thoughts and ideas. The aloneness, the secretiveness and idle hours are a formula for disaster.

Plan Ahead!

When you know that you will be facing some down time, you need to review and refresh your commitment to your Lord, your wife and your A&E Partners before you make the trip. If your commitment is not fresh, firm and sure, your vulnerability will increase dramatically.

Each individual's temptations are unique to that individual; different things trigger different people. To protect himself, a man must have a strategy to keep his mind and hours occupied with intriguing and exciting materials. Planning ahead helps defeat this area of vulnerability.

Here are some suggestions:

- Determine what your "emotional drivers" are.

- Remember that many of us have trained ourselves to use the time when we are alone to keep our sexual lives secret from parents and spouses. Just being alone can trigger tempting images and provide opportunities for inappropriate activities.

- Determine times/circumstances when you are most

vulnerable.

- Make plans to be involved with other Christian men instead of being alone. This is not always possible, but with a little planning and forethought there are opportunities for spiritual growth and encouragement available.

- Avoid the use of alcohol. It will lower your resolve to maintain your commitments.

- Schedule evening workouts. Most hotels have workout rooms that are available in the evenings.

- Research the city you will be traveling to. Locate several churches and investigate what weeknight meetings or Bible studies you could attend. Make some new Christian friends who can help occupy these evenings when you would be alone.

- Visit a Twelve Step Group meeting. In every city there are numerous Twelve Step Groups that provide both growth and relational opportunities.

- Always have a good Christian book with you to read, a tape or CD to listen to or even a video to watch. It should be something exciting and interesting to fill your mind.

- Work on Scripture memorization in the evenings.

- Keep the phone numbers of your A&E Partners close at hand for a spiritual 911 call.

- Got to bed early. Late nights are dangerous.

- Expect God to help you when you commit yourself to purity.

Twelve Step programs urge the participants to be unusually careful at certain times. They have discovered the hard way that we all are most vulnerable to slips, relapses and failures when we are...

- H------hungry.
- A------angry.
- L-------lonely.
- T-------tired.

HALT represents those times when we are most vulnerable and when we need to be most vigilant in our thought lives.

Anger and Temptation

Anger, at all levels of intensity, can be a dangerous factor in coping with temptations. When we are angry at our spouse, ourselves, or at God, that anger cancels out our concerns about the consequences of our choices and behaviors. The more intense the

> *Anger cancels out our concern for consequences.*

anger, the more power it has to override our convictions, values, and even our spiritual commitments. My personal sexual failures were always fueled by anger.

I found a strategy that helped. When I feel angry I try to:

- Admit to myself and to God that I am angry.

- Sit down and write an angry letter to the person I am angry with.

- If the anger is real "hot", I find it helpful to scream into a pillow or to pound the bed with my fists.

- Confess the anger to God in prayer and ask Him to remove the anger. Remember, God has reserved vengeance as His right (Romans 12:19). Vengeance is not a pleasure He has left in our hands.

- Go workout. A good workout, jog or even a walk can be helpful.

Chapter Fourteen talks about A&E Partners. When angry, you can confess your anger to them, listen to their wisdom and ask them to pray for you.

Remember, the anger of man does not bring about the righteous life that God desires (James 1:20).

Self- Condemnation

Self-condemnation is another trap Satan sets up for the un-suspecting. This clever scheme works from two different angles. First, Satan beats you up for allowing yourself to be tempted. "What kind of a Christian are you that you could even think of such a thing?" He begins to attack your self-identity, the freedom and forgiveness you have in Christ. He wants you to get down on yourself because you are able to be tempted. But remember what the Scriptures say: *"Therefore there is now no condemnation for those who are in Christ Jesus."* (Romans 8:1). Remember it is not a sin to be tempted!

> Self-condemnation is a scheme of Satan and has no place in the life of a Christian.

The other angle Satan tries to trip you up with is this lie: "If I hurt bad enough about my sin and if I hurt long enough, then I will be able to avoid the temptation next time. The pain I inflict on myself will keep me from sinning or being tempted again." God does not punish you for sinning. His forgiveness is yours because of the Cross. "And with the temptation God will provide a way of escape." (I Corinthians10:13). And He certainly does not punish you for being tempted. Jesus helps you when you are tempted because He knows what it feels like to face temptation (Hebrews 2:18, 4:15-16).

Self-condemnation is a scheme of Satan and it has no place in the life of a Christian.

Winning over Temptation

When you face temptation and you commit your will to do what the Scriptures say, the Holy Spirit enables you to do what God has asked. But you must take the first step by choosing to obey. Then God acts on your behalf, but you have to make the first move.

> *Satan is the master of deceit and lies. His goal is to get you to fail.*

The temptations that plague you appeal to your sin nature and reveal the possibilities of that nature. Satan is the master of deceit and lies. He presents an option to you with all the sensuous beauty and promises you can imagine. When you say "yes" to his offer, you are saying "no" to God's promises and purpose for your life.

To give up a pleasurable option that Satan offers, you must say "no" to that option. In order to say "no" you

> *In order to say, "NO", you need a bigger "YES"!*

need a bigger "yes". You will not say "no" until you are committed to a bigger and better "yes". This reality takes on special meaning when you are working to break some habit in the sexual arena. Sexual activities are addictive and a person needs a really big "yes" in order to say "no" to the temptations that Satan presents.

Satan's goal is to get you to fail. Once you have failed, he then wants you to conclude that victory cannot be won. The moment you reach the conclusion that victory cannot be won, Satan has gained control over you.

Satan cannot steal your salvation but he can destroy your ministry, your life, your legacy and your family. But when your heart and soul trust God's promises more than the promises of sin, you win. When your heart is filled with God's grace and mercy, there is no room for sin's temptations.

Accountability?

One of the important ways to deal with temptation is the support and encouragement of other Christian men. In Chapter Fourteen, Accountability & Encouragement Partners and Groups are described and a strategy is outlined.

CHAIN BREAKERS

√ Your emotional needs and wounds determine what temptations you are most vulnerable to. Satan attaches his lies to these needs and wounds. Understanding what drives your temptations allows you to choose to overcome them.

√ Learn about and utilize the power of your imagination. Train it to work for God instead of the enemy.

√ Carefully evaluate every thought or idea that comes to mind in light of Scripture; base your evaluation on the Word of God. If you decide to reject a thought or idea as unworthy, you have won that particular battle over temptation.

√ Anger fuels temptation by canceling out your concern for consequences. Deal with your anger issues and take away that tool of Satan.

Chapter Ten

"The Big Issues in the Battle"

There are several big issues that regularly surface in the battle for sexual purity. Some of these issues are quite controversial in different church settings. The information provided here is designed to be helpful and has been thoughtfully prepared over years of counseling experience.

People seem to always be looking for some loopholes in what God says are His sexual boundaries. They want to find some way to have sexual gratification outside of a committed marriage relationship. Satan uses attractive "options" to distract even the most committed Christians. One of the common schemes Satan offers is secrecy.

> *One of the common schemes Satan offers is secrecy.*

Boys Will Be Boys

Your sexual life as a young boy probably developed in secret, hidden away from your parents, particularly from your mother. You were afraid to let anyone know the curious thoughts you had. You knew from whatever behavior you had gotten caught at that Mother did not want you to know about girls and that if she caught you trying to find out, there would be consequences. And if you got caught feeling of yourself there were fears of Daddy being told and even worse consequences. For many of you, there was shame and humiliation about your curious misadventures into the mysteries of sexuality. So secrecy became your friend that both protected you and caused the curiosity to grow.

As you matured, most of you had no one to open up to, no one safe enough to ask curious questions to. So you eavesdropped on the conversations of older boys who seemed to already know what you wanted to know. Your earliest sex education came long before Dad had any kind of "birds and bees" talk with you. But with the teasing/ competitive style of relating that most males grow up with,

> Teasing breeds more secrecy and isolation.

you didn't dare let the guys know what you didn't know. Teasing breeds more secrecy and isolation.

But somehow, by trial and error, sneaking a peak, trying moves, or whatever, most guys finally engage in some sexual activities. By that point, you have developed a "self-assured confidence" mask you wear to hide your fears and doubts. The powerful hormones that you don't understand drive you forward. The images that fill your mind are exciting and fearful. Depending on your religious training or parenting, there often is considerable guilt and shame about wanting to be sexually active and feeling like a failure if you do not at least try.

You sneak a peak at porn at a friend's house. It belonged to his Dad. You swap stories about getting to second base, but don't really understand what's going on. Your sex life is launched, painfully and slowly. Or maybe you are one of the "lucky" guys that gets to be "initiated" by an older

> The conspiracy of silence and lack of understanding about our emotions keep us trapped and imprisoned.

woman or girl. Either way, hidden in secrecy behind implied successes and faked confidences, you grow up a sexual male. Not knowing for sure what you do understand about sexuality and women, but still having no one to talk with, you struggle along.

Few men talk about their feelings or have an opportunity to discuss openly their fears. It is tragic that so many know so little about sexuality as God designed it and yet we have no one to talk to about what we don't know.

This secrecy we learned in childhood continues into

our adult male lives. We men do not talk about sexual things easily with anyone, even our lovers. Performance anxiety, a low level of masculine confidence, and the secrecy we have lived with all of our lives keeps sexual issues and problems hidden in the dark. And this conspiracy of secrecy and lack of understanding about our emotions keep us trapped and imprisoned.

Few men discuss sexual issues and problems unless they are forced to by some pressure in their lives. Their wives "catch" them looking at pornography or some sexual incident becomes public knowledge. This cult of secrecy and isolation is not easily broken because most of us

> **We keep our internal life secret because we are afraid.**

fear, at some deep level, that we are flawed, inadequate or bad. We keep our internal life secret because of the fear.

God wants us all "to walk in the light".

This is the message we have heard from him and declare to you: God is light; in him there is no darkness at all. If we claim to have fellowship with him yet walk in the darkness, we lie and do not live by the truth. But if we walk in the light, as he is in the light, we have fellowship with one another, and the blood of Jesus, his Son, purifies us from all sin. 1 John 1:5-7

The Scriptures tell us, in many passages, that God wants to break this cult of secrecy and fear and wants us to bring all of our secrets to Him. We must walk in the light of God to heal our hearts.

Giving thanks to the Father, who has qualified you to share in the inheritance of the saints in the kingdom of light. For he has rescued us from the dominion of darkness and brought us into the kingdom of the Son he loves.

Colossians 1:12-13

The Church and Sex Education

The Church in general has not offered much help to most men. In fact, most men don't think about the Church as being a source of practical help in most ways, but particularly not in the sexual arena. So Christian men are often in a worse fog about sexual issues than most un-churched men are. Not only do Christian men have limited knowledge, what they do know is layered with even more guilt and shame. Elizabeth Elliot wrote: "It's dangerous and destructive to treat sexuality as if it were meaningless. Much of the church, which is being strongly influenced by the world's ideologues, is ignoring the fact that sexuality means something."

It is time for the Church at large to address the issues of sexuality in a way that is meaningful and helpful for Christians. Today there are some good books being written about healthy sexuality for couples and some good programs designed to teach young people the blessings of abstinence. In general, however, there is still very little material that addresses the real internal issues men are struggling to face.

> It is time for the Church to address sexuality in a way that is meaningful and helpful.

Too often the church in general, and some in particular, are very vocal about what they are against, but not very vocal about what they are for. There is a need to have teaching in the Church concerning healthy relational sexuality. In an attempt to offer some initial help in this area, this book has been written.

The material offered here is aimed at being helpful to men who are struggling, to enable them to break the secrecy barrier that Satan so often uses, and to provide a safe place for guys to begin to discuss their own sexual issues. We are going to look at three main issues of struggle.

Utilize the material you find helpful and, like a good steak dinner, leave the bones on the plate when you finish.

Issue One: Lust

The Scriptures are clear about lust. Jesus enlarged the Jewish laws to include heart attitude and motives with the act of adultery (Matthew 5:27-28). Unfortunately, even this concept has been used to make men feel guilty and shamed. It has been interpreted in such a way that any "noticing" of an attractive person is defined as lustful in some Christian groups. Some men don't have a clue about healthy sexuality so they conclude that any sexual interest or curiosity is sinful. They beat themselves up for the simplest form of sexual attraction. There is no room in their understanding for healthy relational sexuality within God's ordained purposes and boundaries.

> *The Scriptures are clear about lust.*

God desires and intends that His people appreciate the beauty He has created. In Romans it is written that the created world is to picture God's eternal power and divine nature so that people can understand what He is like (Romans 1:20). In Genesis and Psalms it is written that God made a special effort in creating humans (Genesis 2:4-25; Psalm 139:13-16). Certainly some of His finest creative work is seen in the human form. He created men to desire the shapely curves of women and women to desire the physical strength of men. It is appropriate to notice and appreciate beauty, whether it is a beautiful mountain valley or a beautiful person. You can appreciate God's creation without having to possess it, take it home with you.

> *Appreciating beauty is not the same as having to have it.*

If your neighbor has a beautiful flower garden, you can

certainly appreciate the beauty of all the flowers, but it is wrong to want to pick a handful and take them home with you. Appreciating beauty is not the same as having to have it.

The actual translation of the famous verse in Matthew 5:27-28 is "anyone who looks at a woman to lust for her has already committed adultery with her in his heart." When the purpose for looking is to possess, to use for your own sexual fantasy and pleasure, it is lust. Appreciating a beautiful person is appropriate and part of what God built into His creation for our enjoyment.

There is the story of an old English doctor that E. M. Bounds writes about in one of his books on prayer. The good doctor made many house calls in his day and encountered many lovely women in his medical practice. He found it necessary to develop a strategy to help with the issue of lust. So he began to use prayer. When he would encounter a beautiful woman, he would pray for her. He would ask God to make her as beautiful on the inside as she was on the outside and he asked that God would grant her salvation, grace and mercy. Then he would conclude his prayer with gratitude for his own wife that God had so graciously provided for him to meet his needs. He appreciated the woman's beauty but, through prayer, he honored God with His heart attitude.

> When he encountered a beautiful woman, he would pray for her and ask God to make her as beautiful on the inside as she was on the outside.

Issue Two: Masturbation

The majority of males and many females masturbate during their teen and young adult years. Some continue well into mid-life. Many individuals have long-term habitual masturbation issues.

Masturbation is the term used for private sexual release. The purpose here is to present to you a Biblical perspective on your personal sexual issues and provide you with information to enable you to gain self-control in the area of your sexuality.

Remember the Purpose for Sexual Activities

As discussed in Chapter Three, God's ordained purpose for sex is relational, increasing love, intimacy and unity in the marriage relationship with pleasure being the by-product. The world has the perspective that the purpose of sexual activities of any type is for pleasure and that the relational issues are not that important or significant. This is directly the opposite of the Biblical perspective; the Bible makes no provision for sexual activity outside of the marriage relationship because sexual intimacy was created for marriage. (See the World's Perspective vs. the Christian Perspective Chart in Chapter One.)

Scripture clearly states that extra-marital sexual activity is harmful and sinful (I Corinthians 6:9-10, 18; Galatians 5:19-21) and should not be part of a Christian's life. In I Corinthians 7:5,9 one of the stated purposes for sexual intimacy in marriage is to encourage

> *Masturbation can undermine God's purposes for your life.*

self-control. (See "Divine Purposes in our Sexuality" in Chapter Three).

The Bible does not mention masturbation directly in either the Old Testament or New Testament. The Hebraic laws found in Leviticus cover almost every conceivable kind of sexual involvement, but do not mention masturbation. However since masturbation is defined as private sexual release and does not directly encourage intimacy in marriage, it is a sexual behavior that can undermine God's purposes.

147

Is Masturbation Harmful?

Masturbation does not appear to harm a person's body in any way medically, but it does impact a person's attitudes about sex and the purpose for sexual activities. Here are some problems that are often experienced with a long-term habit of masturbation:

• Focus for sexual activity becomes sexual release more than relational connection. Since masturbation is a private sexual release, the importance of relationships is undermined.

• The way a person learns to experience sexual pleasure often determines how he/she will experience sexual pleasures throughout life. Habits that give pleasure are hard to break. The body learns to respond to only one type of stimulation and has difficulty adjusting to normal sexual intercourse.

• Masturbation elevates the physical aspects of sex over the emotional/spiritual aspects. With masturbation, the goal for sexual activity becomes orgasmic pleasure encouraging a "taking" kind of attitude verses a "giving" kind of attitude necessary for loving intimate relationships.

• Masturbation increases the use of inappropriate fantasies in sexual activities and often is connected with or leads to the use of pornography.

• Masturbation becomes a habitual activity and an escape from dealing with the realities of relationships.

• Habitual masturbation leads to sexual dysfunctions

such as pre-mature ejaculation in males and dependence on certain behaviors for orgasmic release in both sexes.

- Masturbation in marriage is a withholding of sexual intimacy from your spouse.

- Masturbation is usually a part of the addictive problem in sexual addictions.

Is Masturbation Ever An Acceptable Behavior?

This is still a controversial topic in certain Christian groups with different Christian leaders landing on different sides of the issue. Personally, I think we have to be very careful in being dogmatic about anything the Scriptures are silent about. I would say that since masturbation involves fantasy, any fantasy that is not focused on your marital partner is lust and sinful. Whatever opinion you have personally, hold it in light of Romans 14:23: "Everything that does not come from faith is sin."

Issue Three: Pornography

Pornography has become a common problem for many Christian men, feeding sexual addictions and destroying marriages and families. It is largely a male problem, but there are some females who use pornography. Pornography is not a new phenomenon since there have been pornographic material discovered in many ancient archeological finds and

> *Pornography is graffiti on the soul.*

ancient literature. But the pervasive use by so many men is a new phenomena and a key factor in sexual addictions.

Pornography is the visual presentation of nudity and sexuality in any form: magazines, drawings, movies, videos, internet websites or cartoon figures. It also includes

> **The law of diminishing returns clearly occurs in the use of pornography.**

the graphic descriptions of sexual activities written in books, magazines or other printed materials. Telephone sex and chat rooms (favored by women) are part of the broad realm of pornographic material.

Some materials may be relatively mild in nature, but are still pornographic and easily lead into other "less mild" materials and activities that are extremely harmful to those who regularly use such materials. The law of diminishing returns clearly occurs in the use of pornography. What was sufficient today for pleasure is not good enough tomorrow, so the person needs more and more and different images.

Pornography is like graffiti on the soul. Your body is the temple of God and when you use pornography, it is like writing graffiti on the walls of that temple. You stain your brain with porn.

A way to conceptualize the impact of pornography is to compare your brain to your car. You wouldn't put sugar in the gas tank of your car, so don't put porn in your brain. Sugar will ruin your car's motor so it won't function right; addiction to pornography will damage the way your brain works.

"What makes pornography so addictive is that more than anything else in a lost man's life, it makes him feel like a man without ever requiring a thing of him. The less a guy feels like a real man in the presence of a real woman, the more vulnerable he is to porn."
John Eldredge, Wild at Heart

Pornography in no way fulfills the Biblical purposes for sexual activities. It is "lust" as defined in the Scriptures:

But I tell you that anyone who looks at a woman lustfully has already committed adultery with her in his heart.
Matthew 5:27

Is Pornography Harmful?

Much research has been conducted on the use of pornography and the answer is a definite "Yes! Pornography is harmful!" Research has linked many sexual issues and even sexual crimes to the habitual use of pornography. For a Christian, pornography is definitely harmful and is a quick pathway to other sexual sins. Here are some of the problems often experienced by those who involve themselves with pornographic material:

- Pornography encourages an unhealthy curiosity and imagination and a hunger to "see" more.

- Pornography gives an unrealistic picture of physical beauty and sexual activities. This contaminates the safety and security of sexual intimacy in marital relationships.

- Pornography feeds all the sexual issues that undermine family values; it destroys families.

- Pornography is often connected to habitual masturbation, so all of the problems related to masturbation also apply to pornography.

- Pornography objectifies women and cheapens the person that Jesus died for.

- Pornography focuses on "body parts" not persons, dehumanizing the person portrayed.

- Pornography gives young girls a wrong perspective about "body-image", what is important concerning feminine beauty and what is appealing to a man.

- Pornography gives men and women wrong perspectives of what is really important in sexual relationships in marriage.

- Pornography promotes the wrong purpose for sexual activity: pleasure instead of relationship.

- Pornography stains the mind and imprints images that are almost impossible to remove.

- Pornography is addicting and a primary component in almost all sexual addictions.

- Pornography (including certain video games), focusing on sadistic and violent sex (rape), has been demonstrated to lead to violence towards women.

- Pornography is a hostile activity and often expresses passive-aggressive hostility toward the sex object as well as passive-aggressive avoidance in the person's relationship with his wife.

- Pornography robs men of time, money and creative energies that could be utilized effectively in their work, marital and family activities.

- Pornography contaminates your personal devotional life and interferes with your personal prayer life.

Satan actively invades the lives of men and women to contaminate the foundations of marriage and family in an attempt to destroy the creative reproductive purposes God ordained for humans. Humans can reproduce life. Satan cannot, and he is angry that men and women can leave a beautiful legacy in their children and grandchildren.

> *Pornography is one of Satan's most enticing tools, designed to work like a spider's web.*

He attacks the basic desires of men and women to reproduce and does everything in his power to destroy the relational foundation that makes leaving a legacy possible. Pornography is one of his most enticing tools designed to work like a spider's web: the prey is attracted by the beauty and, before he knows it, is wrapped up and trapped, the victim of the enemy of his soul.

In Conclusion . . .

There are other issues that men face in dealing with sexual immorality. This discussion covers only three, but the same principles can be applied to other issues.

For example, if your temptations and fantasies involve homosexual images, the same principles apply. Lust, masturbation and pornography feed sexual immorality in homosexual behaviors as they do in heterosexual behaviors.

In Section Four, strategies are provided to enable you to take the information you have learned in Parts One and Two and begin to effectively win the battle. Since immorality begins on the inside – in your heart and soul – only an internal spiritual solution will win the battle. When your heart and soul are transformed, when your understanding of sexuality is reframed and decontaminated from the cultural brine, you will be able to allow God to enable you to walk in purity.

CHAIN BREAKERS

√ Nothing can be healed until your bring it into God's light. Secrets thrive in the dark and can destroy you.

√ Evaluate all of your sexual behaviors with this gauge: Do they lead me closer to God and other Christians or do they isolate me more?

√ There is no web of sin and immorality God cannot overcome. God can and will break the chains that bind you if you sincerely turn to Him for healing.

√ There is nothing casual about your sexuality from God's perspective. Everything sexual connects to your heart and soul.

Part Four

Strategies for Healing

Chapter Eleven

"Restoration and Forgiveness, Hearing the Right Voice"

Mark pulled out his Bible. He had just returned from another sexual encounter. The chemical rush had ceased during his long drive home, and the factors that had motivated his pursuit of sex now seemed distant and so much less powerful than they did just a few hours earlier. A sense of sorrow and shame had crept into his heart and soul. He knew he had done it again. He had broken the vows he made to God to stay pure. He was ashamed and sad.

Mark turned the pages in his Bible to try to find some comfort, some solace for his aching heart. He decided he would use the "shut your eyes and poke" method of Bible reading. He shut the Bible and shut his eyes. He poked his finger into the closed Bible and, where it fell open, he ran his finger down the page with his eyes still closed. His finger stopped. He opened his eyes to see what comfort he might find in the verse where his finger stopped. It read:

"God's name is blasphemed among the Gentiles because of you."
Romans 2:24

Mark dissolved in hot, sobbing tears. He knew this was a message from God. He wept and wailed with deep, wrenching sobs.

Sometimes God does communicate to us through the "close your eyes and poke" method and perhaps He did in this instance. Mark believed he was experiencing what is known as Godly sorrow.

Godly sorrow brings repentance that leads to salvation and leaves no regret, but worldly sorrow brings death.
2 Corinthians 7:10

He felt immense sadness and grief that he had broken

157

his commitment to God about sexual purity and now his heart was breaking. He prayed that God would forgive him and restore him.

When the Spirit of God puts His finger on issues in our lives, we experience a deep grief, a Godly sorrow that aches deep inside. Sometimes He even uses our wounded, overly sensitive conscience from childhood to get our attention. This aching heart is a sure sign that the Spirit of God is moving to free us and heal us from the sin and evil forces that are always pursuing us. Mark was feeling, through sorrow and conviction, the hand of God on his life. One of the sure ways Christians know that God is working in their lives is that when they choose to walk in sin, there is a check inside, an invisible fence that gives us a painful jolt to remind us that we have crossed one of God's boundaries.

> *An aching heart is a sure sign that the Spirit of God is moving to free us and heal us from the sin and evil forces that are always pursuing us.*

I was raised in East Texas and often drove down beautiful country roads through the woods and fields. I was always conscious there were ditches on either side of the road to drain off the water when it rained in the spring and fall. But I also knew that the ditches served another purpose. Since this was a time before four-wheel drive vehicles were common in Texas, the ditches always let drivers know they had run off the road. Now that didn't happen many times, but the ditches always served as a reminder to stay on the road, because it was not an easy or pleasant task to get out of the ditches. We often would send a friend off with a shout of "Keep it between the ditches!"

> **Keep it between the ditches!**

God's boundaries are like those ditches. They remind

us to stay on the road.

Self-Forgiveness and Self-Respect

"Is it really possible?" "It's irreparable!"
"I knew better. I'm a Christian and I did it anyway!"
"Paul may be the worst sinner,
but I'm in the running as the second worst sinner!"
"The relationship can never be restored after what I did!"

Many of us have felt this way at some point in our Christian life. You may be feeling that way right now. Perhaps you have repented and you know that God has forgiven you, but the sense of something being irreparable has caused you to feel hope-

> **God wants to set you free!**

lessly damaged or ruined. Perhaps it is a breech of faith in your marriage relationship or some sexual sin that is too shameful to face. The voices, whether from God or somewhere else, are hammering at you inside.

Whatever it is, all Christians, when they fall into sin, have to face these issues of lost self-respect, guilt, and shame. You are not alone in your inability to feel God's forgiveness and inability to forgive yourself for something that is in your past. You are not alone in trying to silence the other voices. But God wants to set you free.

Oswald Chambers says, *"The sense of the irreparable is one of the greatest agonies in human life."* Satan rejoices when he is able to get a person to that point of feeling hopeless, because at that point they are out of the game as for as Kingdom activity is concerned. Satan's lies destroy your sense of worth and rob you of motivation and energy for Christian service. Satan cannot steal your salvation, but he can sure rob you of your ability to be of service in God's kingdom!

> *Satan cannot steal your salvation, but he can sure rob you of motivation and energy for Christian service.*

So how do you overcome this hopeless feeling that you can never recover from what you have done and you don't deserve to be forgiven? How do you forgive yourself and learn to respect yourself?

The death of Jesus on the Cross reaches into the sense of the irreparable, down beneath the deepest sin we have ever committed and brings forgiveness, reconciliation and healing. The damage we have done can be healed and redeemed through what Jesus did at the Cross and by what the Spirit of God can do in transforming us and those that we have injured. Here are five steps to begin the process of healing:

Step #1:

Renounce your former life and ask God to break all soul ties that bind you to your former life. This is the act of repentance. You turn from your old life and you abstain from your old behaviors. Paul gives a list of activities that the wicked engage in and says:

> *And that is what some of you were. But you were washed, you were sanctified, you were justified in the name of the Lord Jesus Christ and by the Spirit of God.*
>
> 1 Corinthians 6:11

Notice the tense of the verb: "were." It is past tense! When you turn from your sins to Jesus, God does the rest.

Step #2:

As a Christian, confess your sin to God, whatever it

is. Do you really believe what God's Word says about sin, even your sin?

> *If we confess our sins, He is faithful and just and will forgive us our sins and purify us from all unrighteousness.*
>
> 1 John 1:9

This verse clearly states that God forgives all of your sins and purifies you from all unrighteousness. This is true whether you feel forgiven or not. You are forgiven before God. When we confess our sins, the Scriptures teach that God forgives us and restores our purity and innocence.

> *Come now, let us reason together, says the Lord. Though your sins are like scarlet, they will be as white as snow; though they are red as crimson, they shall be like wool.*
>
> Isaiah 1:18

God wants to restore you. He forgives and then He forgets.

> *Their sins and lawless acts, I will remember no more.*
>
> Hebrews 10:17

God intentionally forgets the sins we have committed when we sincerely repent and confess.

> *He does not treat us as our sins deserve or repay us according to our iniquities. For as high as the heavens are above the earth, so great is His love for those who fear Him; as far as the east is from the west, so far as He removed our transgressions from us.*
>
> Psalm 103:10-12

Paul says in his letter to the Romans that there is no condemnation for those in Christ Jesus. God does not hold your sins against you once they are forgiven.

Therefore, there is no condemnation for those who are in Christ Jesus.

Romans 8:1

"God forgives and God forgets" is the line from a popular Christian song, and it is the truth of Scripture. You are forgiven and God does not hold your sins against you in any way. Once you have accepted Christ as your Lord and Savior and confessed your sins, they are forever forgiven and forgotten by God. Read Psalm 51 about David's prayer of confession after his sin with Bathsheba. All of us who have experienced Godly sorrow can identify with David in this Psalm.

Step #3:

After you have studied forgiveness in the passages

| **Give thanks in all circumstances.** |

above, <u>offer a prayer of gratitude to God for His forgiveness.</u> Just a very simple prayer of "Thank You Jesus for dying for my sins" is sufficient if it is heart felt, but some of you might want to write a lengthier prayer like David did in Psalm 51. God is looking at your heart, not just the words you mouth or write. After you pray, read I Thessalonians 5:18:

Give thanks in all circumstances, for this is God's will for you in Christ Jesus.

I Thessalonians 5:18

This reinforces the prayer you just finished praying. Now take it a step further. Have you thanked God for the circumstances and consequences involved in and around your sin?

Notice that this verse includes everything, even the circumstances and consequences of your sin. How can you thank God for the consequences of your sins? You can give thanks because God is so big He can make even the worst consequence of your sin work out for good.

"And we know that in all things God works for the good of those who love Him, who have been called according to His purpose."
Romans 8:28

When you give thanks to God for the forgiveness of your sins, you will often feel forgiven and be able to forgive yourself.

To assist you in seeing God's grace and mercy in these areas, ask Him to show you how He might use your sins or how He could possibly cause the consequences of your sins to work out for good. If you have A & E partners (Chapter Fourteen) ask them to help you see ways God has worked something good through your sins and their consequences. Make a list of what God shows you.

> *Have you thanked God for the circumstances and consequences involved in and around your sin?*

For example, one way God works something good through the consequences of your situation is that He uses what you learn to minister to others.

Praise be to the God and Father of our Lord Jesus Christ, the Father of compassion and the God of all comfort, who comforts us in all our troubles, so that we can comfort those in any trouble with the comfort we ourselves have received from God.
2 Corinthians 1:3-5

God comforts you so you can have a ministry of comfort to others.

163

Step #4:

One other step may be needed to help you <u>truly forgive</u> <u>yourself:</u>

Therefore, confess your sins to each other and pray for each other so that you may be healed. The prayer of a righteous man is powerful and effective.

James 5:16

Sometimes, forgiveness is easier to accept when you experience it fleshed out by another person. You may read and understand that God forgives you, but having another person voice forgiveness and acceptance may be the key for you to feel forgiven.

> **Sometimes forgiveness is easier to accept when you experience it fleshed out by another person.**

Many times the fact of another's acceptance of you, while not condoning your sin, helps you be more accepting of yourself. There may be some other significant person in your life that you also may feel a need to confess your sin to. Perhaps it is a spiritual mentor, spouse or even a parent. Talk with your A & E Partners and see if they can help you explore who you might want to go to with your confession, if anyone.

Step #5:

Depending on the sin and the persons involved, <u>restitution or amends</u> might be appropriate. Discuss this possibility with your A&E Partners and be very careful to allow the Spirit of God to guide you.

Here are some questions to consider:

- Why do you want to confess to this person?

- Is this the right time for confession?

- Can the person handle the truth at this point in his/her life?

- Does someone need to go with you for the confession?

- Are you really hearing God's voice or some other voice?

Hearing the Right Voice

Some of us, when we continue to struggle with self-acceptance and forgiveness, are battling an overly sensitive or wounded conscience. This was the case with Mark, the story from the beginning of the chapter. Mark had grown up in a home where his mother was particularly shaming about anything sexual and he developed a deep sense of shame in his own life. When he violated his super sensitive conscience, he was overwhelmed with guilt and shame. He could not distinguish between God's voice convicting him with Godly sorrow and Satan's voice taking advantage of his wounded conscience.

Intimacy with God and walking in purity involves hearing His voice, just as love and intimacy develop on the human level as we talk and listen with each other. The words we use, the tone of voice, and the volume of our interactions all communicate our feelings to one another. In the same way, as we listen to God's voice and become familiar with His words, His tone and attitude, we learn to draw close to Him. We become familiar with His voice and when He

> *As we listen to God in our Christian walk, His Spirit begins to identify those other voices that are not from Him.*

165

calls our name, we immediately recognize and respond. As we listen to God in our Christian walk, His Spirit begins to identify those other voices that are not from Him.

Scolding from God?

I remember coming home from a date in high school and being a little late. I was fearful of being scolded by my mother and father. The term "scold" is not a term that we hear very often in today's society, but it means a harsh rebuke. I was afraid of the harsh rebuke I was going to get from my parents. I

> *Many Christians have an unhealthy fear God will scold them when they come to Him after a sexual failure.*

knew that I would still be their son, but I hated being scolded. It always stirred feelings of shame.

Many Christians have an unhealthy fear God will scold them when they come to Him after a sexual failure. They hunger to be loved and accepted by God, but they fear His harsh rebuke, even His rejection. And in their head and heart they may hear the voice of a wounded sensitive conscience, overly strict parent or some religious authority. So they quickly say a silent confession in their heads, if they confess at all, and quickly try to forget the failure.

We all want to bury this sense of failure, the guilt and shame, so we stuff it into our unconscious. For many of us there is no sense of purging and cleansing. There is no awareness of being forgiven. All we hear are condemning voices.

Most of us feel grateful for busyness and an occupied mind so we don't have to feel guilt and shame about the failure or hear the voices. We tell ourselves "rational lies" such as: "Everyone's doing it." "Hey, I'm only human." "It won't happen again." It's amazing how these rationalizations we make to ourselves after a sexual failure sound like the same excuses we tried to make with our mothers and fathers.

Mark had reached the point of Godly sorrow. He knew that he was in the ditch and he was begging God to help him get out of the ditch and stay out. The Bible verse he read, although painful, did not cause shame. Our Lord will speak truth to us, but never in a condemning way.

Our Heavenly Father does not scold us as our earthly parents perhaps did. When we turn from our sin He has compassion on us, runs to meet us and embraces us (Luke 15:20).

His Sheep Hear His Voice

In John 10:3, it is written that "the sheep" hear the Shepherd's voice and the Shepherd calls them by name. God uses our name to call to us. He calls and we hear. Those other voices we hear (our wounded consciences, our internalized parenting messages, the world and Satan) are calling to us also, but usually they use other terms than our name.

Have you ever heard these words?

"Hey, stupid! Yeah, you dummy!"
"There you go again; you are just a royal screw-up!"
"You've really done it this time!"
"You are a sex addict and you always will be."
"You are hopeless!"

Such words as "lazy, stupid, dumb, pervert, loser, no-good, selfish, ugly, mean" and many, many more are not terms that a loving Shepherd uses. Remember He has forgiven your sin and then forgotten your sin. He is not the accuser and His voice does not bring shame and guilt.

What Name Do You Hear?

Listen for your name. The Good Shepherd calls you by name (John 10:3; Isaiah 43:1). John 10:4 says the sheep "know" His voice. In the Greek, this is the word that means to know by experience. It means the sheep are familiar with the Shepherd's voice because they have heard it many times before. Verse 5 says the sheep are not familiar with the voice of strangers; they do not recognize the other voices. By being with the Shepherd, the sheep have learned how to recognize His voice. There is no substitute for familiarity with the Shepherd.

If we are going to walk in purity and be free from condemnation, we must learn to distinguish the Good Shepherd's voice from all the other intrusive messages that find their way into our heads.

Here are some guidelines to distinguish between the voice of God and the voices Satan uses to distract, deceive and destroy us.

God's Voice	Satan's Voice
1. God calls to us with the gentle loving voice of a Shepherd, creating peace.	1. Satan's voices accuse, threaten, intimidate, demand, creating fear and chaos.
2. The Lord's voice is internal, quiet and lovingly gentle.	2. Satan's voices are intrusive, distracting, confusing.
3. God always speaks in ways that agree with Biblical principles.	3. Satan uses Scripture out of context.

God's Voice	Satan's Voices
4. God's voice is always true to the revealed attributes of God.	4. Satan calls God's attributes and character into question. ("If God really loved you...")
5. God's voice is filled with mercy and grace. There is no condemning tone (Romans 8:1).	5. Satan's voices create feelings of worthlessness, hopelessness, and condemnation.
6. God's voice focuses on changing us.	6. Satan points to others as being the problem and who we need to change.
7. God's voice focuses on truth and hope.	7. Satan's voices remind us of failures, mistakes, negative experiences.
8. God's voice focuses on the here and now rather than on past or future. ("Don't worry about tomorrow." Matt. 6:34)	8. Satan's voices cause us live in the past ("If only...") or future ("What if...").
9. God's counsel is usually simple and practical.	9. Satan's voices suggest impractical and complicated schemes.
10. God's words are usually about the ordinary and mundane in contrast to always being spectacular..	10. Satan's voices appeal to our fleshly desires to be spectacular, seeking approval from others and applause.

God's Voice	Satan's Voice
11. God's voice increases our hope.	11. Satan's voices rob us of hope.
12. When we hear God's voice, we have more empathy for others.	12. Satan's voices want us to despise, envy and compete.
13. God's voice brings peace even when outward circumstances do not change.	13. Satan's voices increase our ingratitude, dissatisfaction, and anxiety.

Hearing God's voice is always easier when our heart response is a willingness to be obedient. God's Spirit in us is always in tune to the Father's heart and mind, bringing to us all that is in the Father's heart and mind about us. Satan's voices are most distracting when they find hesitancy within us towards obedience, particularly in the sexual arena of our lives.

> *Hearing God's voice is always easier when our heart response is a willingness to be obedient.*

To clearly distinguish God's voice, there must be a willingness to obey whatever His word might be. We need to listen for the voice of the Father continually and the moment we hear, we are to yield to Him in obedience. As we listen for God's Word we are to trust Him to clarify His Word spoken to us and trust Him to enable us to remember what He says (John 16:13-15).

The God of Restoration

God wants to restore us and He wants us to hear His voice. He wants us to be free from condemnation, shame and guilt. God never intended for you or any person to

170

continue to suffer once he has put His faith in Christ's atoning sacrifice and made peace with God. The lies of Satan are usually the major issues that contaminate your feelings.

He tells you lies about God the Father and His character; he tells you lies about yourself, about other people and how these people may view you. He also tells you lies about how your sins will forever stain your life. Remember God is the God of restoration. With God, nothing is impossible. God invented the concept of recycling and restoration. This includes forgiveness of the worst sins and restoration of your self-respect.

CHAIN BREAKERS

√ Godly sorrow keeps us between the ditches!

√ Confess your sins to God with a repentant heart attitude.

√ God forgives the sin, forgets the sin and restores your innocence.

√ Give God thanks because He will use the consequences of your sins for your good and His glory.

√ Distinguish between the kind voice of the Shepherd and the condemning voices of Satan.

Chapter Twelve

"Transformation & Healing of Memories"

Tommy was a pilot in his late 40's. He had a problem with anxiety and fear, and he was concerned it would create problems with his career.

He began to see a psychiatrist for treatment of anxiety and panic disorder. For several years, he took the prescribed meds and talked to a professional counselor. He dealt with his childhood experiences of having a violent father who abandoned the family when he was young.

Tommy came to my office several years after the first panic attack. He said that he was still struggling with fears and anxiety and felt the medicines were not helping. As we talked, he admitted to an on-going anger problem and sexual issues he had never dealt with. Tommy wanted God to heal him at a deeper level.

The process that God uses to heal our emotional wounds is called transformational healing. Through this growth process, God brings healing to His children. I am still involved in this process and, by His grace and through the power of the Holy Spirit, He is transforming me to be like Christ. This is what He is doing with all of us who put our faith in Jesus (II Corinthians 3:18; Galatians 4:19; Ephesians 4:12). This is what I mean when I write "winning is an inside job".

Our emotional wounds are similar to physical cuts or wounds on our body. A cut on the arm can become contaminated and infected with bacteria or germs. A painful infection can follow. Antibiotics are applied and the germs and bacteria are killed.

> **Heart and soul wounds can become infected, too.**

Heart and soul wounds can become contaminated and infected, too. It is not germs and bacteria that infect heart and soul wounds, but rather the lies of Satan. We ask God to apply His antibiotic (His truth found in the Scriptures) to the wounds and kill the lies. This is the way the healing and transformational process works. Without this transformational healing, there is no long-term victory. Tommy was seeking healing at a deeper level.

Tools for Transformation
The Holy Spirit uses two tools to transform us.

• He uses the Word of God. The Scriptures are the source of God's Truth that combats Satan's lies.

• He uses other believers in loving relationships to make the Word of God real in flesh and blood terms. I can read about God's love in the Scriptures, but when I feel the love of another Christian, God's love becomes real in my life. When God wants me to understand His love and His character, He always incarnates that Truth in a person, someone with "skin on".

Each individual has to intentionally choose to submit himself to God's transformational healing process. God does not force you to find healing, but He allows you to reap the consequences of your choices
(Galatians 6:7-8) until you hurt so bad that you want to be healed. You get to choose to involve yourself in His healing process. As you are transformed by God's Spirit, you will be enabled to maintain sexual purity.

Responsibility?
What does God hold you accountable for? This question is important because one of the enemy's tricks is to get you to think you are responsible for things that God

does not hold you accountable for. The flip side to that trick is to blame your issues (things you are responsible for) on another person.

God holds you accountable for those things you can control, those issues that originate from inside your heart and soul. He does not expect you to make every one happy, to fix everyone's problems, or to

> *God holds you accountable for those things you can control, those issues that originate from inside your heart and soul.*

control things outside of your realm of authority. You are responsible for the choices you make, your reactions to things that happen and to the way you treat others. Those closest to you are usually the best mirrors of what you are truly like. Your reactions to these people are God's way of showing you what is still messed up in your heart, what you have not dealt with, what your unfinished business is.

One of God's greatest gifts to you as a human being is your mind, the ability to think, reason and remember. It is so complex that researchers still only know a tiny bit of what it is capable of doing. Your mind remembers everything you have ever experienced, done, said, thought and felt. Your life history is recorded and marked deep inside your memory. If you could slice your memory open like a logger slices a tree, you could see your history much like you can see a tree's history from the rings in the trunk of the tree. God has structured the growth process in such a way that you become who you are through the experiences of your life. He uses your life experiences as teaching and training devices to make you more like Christ.

Why History Is Important

To understand how God uses your history, you can look at how He instructed the nation Israel to use their history. He didn't tell them to forget what they had experienced,

> *God delivers you from your afflictions; He comforts you so you can comfort others.*

but to enshrine their history with festivals and feasts to remind them of His great deliverances and as a teaching device for their children (Exodus 12:14,26-27; Joshua 4:4-7 and many other places). He even · says we are to learn from their history (I Corinthians 10:6,11-13).

Paul says in II Corinthians 1:3-5 that God comforts you in all your afflictions so that you will have a message of comfort for others. Often people think that this refers only to a current experience of God's comfort. It is also true of your history. God has delivered you from your afflictions and you have been comforted so you can comfort others. Isn't this what the "word of our testimony" (Revelation 12:11) means: the story of how God has worked in your life to deliver you from your sin and your painful memories?

When you refuse to look at your history, you are limit-

> *When you refuse to look at your history, you are limiting what God has given you.*

ing what God has given you. God has allowed you to have the history you have so you can minister His mercy and grace through your story. The "word of our testimony" that overcomes the evil one (Revelation 12:11) is your story of how God has transformed you. When you refuse to look at your history and feel all your pain, you are not allowing God to have all of you for all of His purposes. You say Romans 8:28 is true about what happens to you today, but are you willing to say it is true for your history as well? God uses everything that has ever touched your life for His purposes if you allow Him to. You have nothing to fear if you know He is really in control.

"All things" include life circumstances, bad choices,

mistakes, overt sin, times you were a victim, times when you were an abuser; even things like abusive parents, Viet Nam experiences and painful divorce experiences. Flippantly saying, "I've given that to the Lord," without processing His healing is, in reality, saying, "I don't believe that God can use that for anything good today."

God wants you to let Him have all those feelings and allow Him to work in you and through you in all these areas. Whatever experiences you have ever had that you do not allow Him to work in, and through, is an area that will contaminate your life experiences and relationships. These areas are also like un-mined treasures that can never be used to benefit others.

When you own and accept your history as a gift from God (Psalm 139:16) and allow Him to heal those deepest hurts and wounds, He transforms you on the inside so that you are more like Christ. He heals those issues that cause you to react and over-react inappropriately. You truly become like Christ on the inside! His transforming love, grace, mercy and forgiveness take the most horrible, shameful, degrading experiences and turn them into part of your story ("word of our testimony") that He uses to comfort and help others. That's the way God does it. You can call it "healing of memories", you can call it "counseling" or "soaking prayer". God takes your worst and makes it His best! And in every case, He uses other people in the Body of Christ and His Word (Scriptures) to transform you (Romans 12:1-2).

> *God takes your worst and makes it His best.*

The Healing of Memories

There are depths within every person that he/she does not comprehend. God has so structured humans and their abilities have been so damaged by the Fall that they are unable to plumb these depths without help from His Spirit. Jeremiah said:

The heart is deceitful above all things and beyond cure. Who can understand it?

Jeremiah 17:9

Jesus said that out of our heart comes sexual immorality and evil (Matthew 15:19; Mark 7:21) and that nothing is hidden that will not be revealed (Luke 8:17,12:2-3). The question then is how does God reveal you to yourself? If you cannot know your own heart, because your heart deceives you not others, how do you get to know what is deep inside? How do you heal your heart and soul if you are unconscious of the wounds?

> **There are depths within every person that he/she does not comprehend.**

Work of the Spirit

The Holy Spirit reveals you to yourself. Only with God's help can you understand the depths of your heart and certainly you cannot grow spiritually without the Spirit intervening. Paul says that men can plant and water, but only God makes you grow (I Corinthians 3:5-9). The Spirit of God is unlimited in His ability to touch your life and He uses numerous unlimited ways to teach you about yourself. The only requirement is for you to be willing to learn and grow, to be teachable, allowing the Spirit of God to show you what

He wants you to know (John 16:13). You must be willing to submit to God's process and be willing to obey what God shows you.

Tommy prayed that day in my office and asked the Holy Spirit

to touch his life and guide him into a better understanding of why he was so fearful and angry. When he finished the prayer, I asked him what he thought God was saying to him. Tommy indicated that one word kept coming to mind. He told me what the word was, and it had to do with where he had lived as a child. As he began to talk, all the details began to pour out and he began to cry.

He told of the lower class neighborhood he grew up in and how his mother always had men around after her husband abandoned the family. The tears became anger, and he poundd his leg with his fist.

Over the next hour, God flushed out numerous childhood memories as I let Tommy talk. His disgust, shame and anger at his mother poured out his mouth with words and out of his eyes with tears. The Holy Spirit was beginning to heal his memo-ries.

Where Do We Start?

The beginning step in the healing of memories is to make Psalm 139:23-24 your heart-prayer to the Lord:

Search me, O God, and know my heart; Test me and know my anxious thoughts. See if there is any offensive way in me, and lead me in the way everlasting.

Psalm 139:23-24

Solomon wrote in Proverbs:

The lamp of the Lord searches the spirit of man; it searches out his inmost being.

Proverbs 20:27

When you make this your heart-prayer and you are willing to allow God's Spirit to teach you what He wants to teach you, you can expect God to open your eyes to see what He wants to accomplish in your life. **This process**

is about your seeing what God wants you to see so you can become who God wants you to be. God wants you to become like Christ on the inside (manifest the fruit of the Spirit from an inner Christ-likeness). He often uses our closest relationships (wife and children) to reveal those areas where you are not yet like Christ.

Tommy shared with me that his wife had told him on several occasions that he had an anger problem. As he shared, God enabled him to see how his anger and his exposure to his mother's sexual issues had contaminated his life and marriage.

Hidden Garbage Pits

When you have areas of your life that are hidden and unexplored, areas that you have been unwilling to deal with for whatever reason, they are like "garbage pits" that create all sorts of problems for you. Primarily these garbage pits contaminate (stink up) your relationships. You may be totally unaware of how this is happening because you tend to deceive yourself (Jeremiah 17:9). God allows others to see these areas; you do not deceive them even when you think you are hiding these garbage pits. The Lord says that all of these areas in your life and in everyone else's life will be brought into the light.

There is nothing concealed that will not be disclosed, or hidden that will not be made known. What you have said in the dark will be heard in the daylight, and what you have whispered in the ear in the inner rooms will be proclaimed from the housetops.

Luke 12:2-3

Tommy allowed God's light to shine on his childhood memories and he began to experience the deeper healing he desired. God freed him from his fears and sexual struggles as he forgave his mother and father.

The Power of His Light

God brings everything into the light (Hebrews 4:13; Luke 8:17). It is only in the light that you find healing and forgiveness (I John 1:7,9). Only that which is externalized from your secret life can be exposed to the light. God wants to clean up all these garbage pits wherever and whatever they may be. Unexposed secrets create all kinds of problems and fears in your lives ("If they knew about this or that, they will not love me and certainly will not allow me to minister.") and become entry points for all sorts of satanic attack. Every garbage pit is like a land mine, just waiting for you to step on (or in!). John writes:

> *There is no fear in love. But perfect love drives out fear because fear has to do with punishment. The man who fears is not made perfect in love.*
>
> 1 John 4:18

We sometimes hear Christian men talk about "turning on the lights and watching the cockroaches run" when they deal with Satanic forces. Demons can't hang around in the light. James and Peter both tell you to resist Satan and he will flee (James 4:7; I Peter 5:9). The greatest deterrents you have against the enemy are truth and light.

> *If we walk in the light as He is in the light, we have fellowship with one another, and the blood of Jesus, His Son, purifies us from every sin.*
>
> 1 John 1:7

A Personal Challenge

You have a hunger and thirst to be right with God, to see His face, to be used mightily by God. You are a man who wants to do what

> God is putting His finger on some issues in your life that He wants to heal.

God wants you to do. God is putting His finger on some issues in your life that He wants to heal. He loves you and has called you. You are right where God wants you to be. He wants to accomplish a deeper work in you to heal those garbage pits and free you from the issues that cause your life to be a mess. You can have a support system like you have never had before…men who love you and will pray for you and stand with you no matter what issues you have to face. Now is the time to face all the issues you have been running from.

CHAIN BREAKERS

√ Everything that has life grows. God intends for you to grow through a transformational process. Commit yourself to God's process.

√ Emotional wounds get infected by Satan's lies. Ask God to cancel out the lies with His truth and to heal your emotional wounds.

√ There are depths within your heart and soul that only God can plumb. Ask God to dredge your soul and heal anything that hinders your relationship with Him.

√ Allow God to teach you through your personal history.

√ Now is the time for your healing.

Chapter Thirteen

"Understanding Sexual Purity"

Purity is not about perfection. It is about experiencing a process of being purified. God is the master of this process; you are the one needing to be purified.

It is important you understand that purity is not an absence of sexual thoughts and feelings. Purity is what happens when you live with your sexuality as God intended:

- Viewing all persons as individuals who God loves, individuals valued and treasured by Him.

- Understanding the purposes of your sexuality as ordained by God.

- Valuing your sexuality as a picture of God's creative process and a picture of the way He desires to relate to every person.

- Expressing your sexuality within the bonds and boundaries of a covenant marriage relationship.

- Experiencing God's healing for your woundedness and His forgiveness of your sexual sins.

Why Walk in Sexual Purity?

As men we desire to fix everything, even our own lives. One of the ways we work at fixing things is to try and understand the bottom line behind the issues. Why do we need to fix this area of sexual purity in our lives? Our motivation to change our lives increases when we know the reasons why something is important. Here is a partial list of reasons (the bottom line) why we as adult males need to walk in sexual purity.

- It is God's desire for us to walk in sexual purity. The information in this book gives you lots of information from Scriptures indicating that God wants His people to live a life of purity, particularly in the sexual area (I Thessalonians 4:3-8; I Corinthians 6:18-20).

- Walking in purity prepares you to experience the greatest fulfillment and maximum joy in your life as husband and father. God's purposes and His boundaries are to protect your relationships and your marriage from the painful consequences and destruction that accompany immorality.

- Walking in purity is evidence of your maturity. A mature man can control himself sexually outside of marriage and he can express himself in healthy ways sexually in his marriage relationship.

- Walking in purity builds your self-control and strengthens it in other areas of your life. A lack of self-control in one area generalizes over time to other areas in your life.

- Walking in purity builds trust in your relationships and enables you to have trust in your marriage. If you know that you have the ability to control yourself sexually, it makes it easier for you to believe that your spouse is trustworthy. It also enables your spouse to feel cherished and special; it enables her to trust you.

- Walking in purity protects you and your family from sexually transmitted diseases. This is true even if you are single because some STDs are forever. A single person can get an STD and pass it on to his wife and children when he marries.

- Walking in purity builds trust which protects you, your spouse and children from emotional wounds and trauma related to immorality.

- A life of purity prepares you to raise children who walk in purity and to teach them how to protect themselves from sexual immorality.

- Walking in purity simplifies life. Purity protects you from consequences, guilt, shame, regret and fears.

- Purity frees you from distractions that steal your time, energy and money.

- Purity keeps your imagination free and open before God and keeps the enemy from stealing your creativity.

- Walking in purity enables you to live a life of spiritual boldness and frees you to make a difference for God.

My personal life experiences and forty years of ministry and counseling experience confirm the truth of these statements. I whole-heartedly challenge you to heed the words of Paul to Timothy:

Flee the evil desires of youth, pursue righteousness, faith, love and peace along with those who call on the Lord out of a pure heart.
2 Timothy 2:22

A Definition of Purity

A simple definition for purity is: walking clean before God. To walk clean before God is to walk in His light, allowing it to shine into your heart and soul so that you are transparent before the Lord. Your

> **Purity is not about perfection!**

187

internal motivations, as well as your behaviors, are open to His scrutiny. Purity is not about perfection. It is about being right with God by being clean and free from sexual immorality. Purity, as we are using the concept, is a purity of heart and motive as well as purity in behavior. This idea of purity is a rare perspective in today's culture.

> *A simple definition of purity is walking clean before God.*

Webster's Dictionary defines "pure" as "free from moral fault or guilt; marked by chastity." In the New Testament, the Greek word means "clean, pure, and clear". In a spiritual sense, it means free from the pollution and guilt of sin (Matthew 5:8; John 13:10-11 15:3; I Timothy 1:5, 3:9; James 1:27). The word is closely related to the concept of purging and it has the same root from which the English word "catharsis" comes from.

"Catharsis" is an emotional, internal cleansing by purging of feelings. It is used in counseling when a person releases emotional energy in a spontaneous outpouring of tears, grief or anger. The person's soul is purified from unwanted, painful feelings.

Understanding Purity

Perhaps it will help you understand the concept of purity by using an analogy from the physical realm. Are you familiar with the process of water purification?

Purified water is water that has had anything "un-pure" (impurities) removed from it. It is not just visible pollutants that are removed, but also pollutants that cannot be seen by the naked eye. Purification is the process of removing anything that would make the water harmful to drink. Purified water has been through the process of being purified; usually this means either a distilling or chemical process.

The removal of harmful pollutants makes the water more "usable". This means it is safer to drink. Paul used an analogy in II Timothy that illustrates spiritual purification for similar reasons:

> *In a large house there are not only articles of gold and silver, but also of wood and clay; some are for noble purposes and some for ignoble. If a man cleanses himself from the latter, he will be an instrument for noble purposes, made holy, useful to the Master and prepared to do any good work.*
>
> 2 Timothy 2:20-21

To be pure (and safe for use) water must go through the process of being purified. After being purified once, it needs to be kept pure by the way it is stored and used. If you mix purified water with unpurified water, all the water becomes polluted. Just a few

> *You cannot be holy without being pure, and you will be pure if you are holy.*

drops of polluted water can pollute a whole bottle or even a tank of pure water. All the water becomes unusable (polluted) because of a tiny bit of unpure water being mixed with it. The whole tank must be purified again.

In spiritual terms, purification means the removal of anything that is sinful, anything that falls short of God's character and standard. God has removed your sins and everything that polluted your life at the Cross. He desires to remove from your life daily anything that hinders you from being more like Christ. At the Cross, you were purified by the blood of Christ and now you choose to walk in purity "by obeying the truth" (1 Peter 1:22).

The concepts of purity and holiness are first cousins theologically. You cannot be holy without being pure and you will be pure if you are holy. "Holy" has the sense of being dedicated and set apart for God; "purity" is used to describe the character of life a "holy" person lives. If you have truly given your life over to the Lordship of Christ, then your life will be characterized by purity.

Strategies to Maintain Sexual Purity

Purification is not so much about what you do as it is about what you experience. When you intentionally submit yourself to the process that God has ordained for your growth and transformation, you will learn to walk in purity.

> *The Holy Spirit utilizes God's Word and relationships with God's people to transform your life.*

The Holy Spirit utilizes God's truth (His Word) and relationships with His people to transform your life. When you intentionally participate in studying the Scriptures and interacting with your fellow Christians, you will be transformed and you will begin to walk in purity a little more each day.

You were washed, you were sanctified and you were justified (I Corinthians 6:11). You have been given Christ' righteousness (II Corinthians 5:21) and you are now white as snow (Isaiah 1:18). Since you have been purified, you can now walk in purity. God has cleaned you up, and now He will enable you to walk in purity.

But if we walk in the light, as He is in the light, we have fellowship with one another, and the blood of Jesus, His son, purifies us from every sin.

1 John 1:7

The term "walk" is used in a figurative manner to mean your daily way of life or your ordinary daily behavior. When you walk in the light, you are walking in wisdom and obedience, consciously aware of the presence of God each step of your day. You walk with God who loves you, wants you free and who can free you.

Steps to Maintain a Daily Walk in the Light

STEP #1: <u>Begin each day with a personal time with the Lord.</u>

Begin each day with a fresh commitment to stay in the light and to walk in purity. One of the best ways to do this is to begin each morning with a personal time to focus yourself on God's presence, to remind yourself that you always live "coram deo, in the presence of God". He has said He will never leave you nor forsake you (Hebrews 13:5) and even if you have been unfaithful, He remains faithful and He will not disown you (II Timothy 2:13).

STEP #2: <u>Ask God to reveal to you the emotional issues or wounds that have energized your sexual urges</u> (Psalm 139:23-24).

You may have discovered some of these issues already in your life. Perhaps, as you have read this book, you have identified additional issues. Continue to pray and ask God to show you the wounds you have and the lies you have believed. Ask God to reveal His truth that counters these lies. You often need to have one or two trusted persons to help you see what God wants to heal. Remember that the heart is deceitfully wicked and that the person it deceives is you. Your Christian brothers are valuable allies and their encouragement is essential (Hebrews 10:25).

> *You often need one or two trusted friends to help you see what God wants to heal.*

The Scriptures teach that you must resist Satan in all of his lies (1 Peter 5:8, James 4:7) and take all of these thoughts captive (2 Corinthians 10:3-5). You can break soul ties through repentance, confession and by renouncing them in the name of Jesus. Once you have broken them, you can defeat the flashback memories, when a person comes to mind, by praying for the person and thanking God that He has set you free.

STEP #3: <u>Practice personal discipline in other areas of your life.</u>

When a person practices personal self-discipline in any area of his life, it makes it easier to practice discipline in other areas. Many who struggle with undisciplined sex lives lack discipline in other areas as well.

STEP #4: <u>Get off the roof!</u>

This concerns avoiding situations that are tempting and is based on the story of King David we discussed in Chapter Nine. We read in 2 Samuel that David was walking on his roof when he saw Bathsheba bathing on a roof nearby. Instead of getting off the roof, he stayed and fell into immorality. Many of us have experienced something similar in our own lives. We faced a temptation, but instead of getting up and walking away, we began to play with the idea in our minds and ended up succumbing to the temptation. So get off the roof! The Scriptures tell men to run from lust (2 Timothy 2:22) and pursue those things that produce Godliness and purity.

STEP# 5: <u>Practice prayer instead of lust!</u>

In his letter to Timothy, Paul admonished him to treat younger women as sisters with absolute purity (1 Timothy 5:2). Each person is a living soul that is precious to Jesus, a person He died for at the Cross. You are to treat every-one with respect because they are valuable and precious to God.

A simple process to do this is to practice CPR for Lust:

- <u>Consider who the person is in God's eyes:</u> a human soul wrapped in skin who is precious to God, a person Jesus died for.

- <u>Pray for the person.</u> You short-circuit lust by praying for the person instead of lusting for that person. When you see a beautiful person, take the opportunity to say a prayer for her:

  "Father God, you sure did a beautiful job on that person! I pray that you make her as beautiful on the inside as she on the outside. Thank you that I can trust you to provide for all my personal needs through my wife."

  Most men find it hard to see a woman as precious to God, pray for that woman and then lust after her. Gaining God's perspective of the other person changes sinful agendas. A young pastor I trained years ago recently informed me that he still uses this prayer quite often to maintain God's perspective. He is not alone; so do I.

- <u>Remember who you are in Christ.</u>

  Keeping your perspective about who you are (a container for God's Spirit) and how God is committed to taking care of His own, refocuses your sense of self-worth.

STEP # 6: <u>Participate in an A&E Partnership and an A&E Group designed for accountability and encouragement.</u> (This is covered in more detail in a separate manual by the same name.)

CHAIN BREAKERS

√ Choose to walk in purity and reap the benefits of a clean life.

√ Practice CPR for Lust. It breaks the bondage of your eyes and your heart.

√ Get off the roof! Flee from temptation. If David could fall into immorality, so can you.

√ Don't try to walk in purity alone. It will not work. You need your Christian brothers to stand with you.

Chapter Fourteen

"Accountability and Encouragement"

(A&E Partnerships and Groups)

²³Let us hold unswervingly to the hope we profess, for he who promised is faithful. ²⁴And let us consider how we may spur one another on toward love and good deeds. ²⁵Let us not give up meeting together, as some are in the habit of doing, but let us encourage one another —and all the more as you see the Day approaching.

Hewbrews 10:23-25

Winning the battle and walking in purity is an inside job, but it is not a job that can be done alone. As said throughout this book, God has ordained the Holy Spirit to utilize two key tools for your growth and maturity:

The Word of God
and
The People of God

When you intentionally study God's Word, the Holy Spirit takes that Truth and applies it to your life in the context of authentic relationships with His people. It is God's Truth, revealed and understood by the power of the Holy Spirit (John16:13) and lived out in relationships with God's people, that transforms your life (Romans 12:1-2).

Accountability and Encouragement Partnerships and Groups are designed to create authentic relationships in which you can be transformed. Your participation in A&E

Partnerships and Groups will assist you in developing a mature walk in purity. A&E Partnerships and Groups are designed to function within the local church structure and should enhance your church experience, not distract from it.

Accountability Is Not the Emphasis!

A major reason for changing the paradigm of accountability partnerships to A&E Partnerships is to establish a relational focus as the primary ingredient. Accountability is not as effective when relationships are not healthy and well developed. Too often problems occur in relationships or groups that focus on accountability and foster unhealthy relational issues or tendencies. These problems have become the cause of the early demise of many accountability partnerships.

Reasons Why Traditional Accountability Partnerships Might Not Work

1. The focus on accountability promotes a hierarchal structure and often allows men to slip into defensive-control posturing rather than an open mutual vulnerability.

2. Sometimes men hide behind their leadership skills that enable them to avoid having to deal with issues in their own lives. Healthy relationships help take the competitive issues out of the interaction.

3. Men may fall into the trap at times of trying to fix their partners instead of building healthy relationships and allowing God to work.

4. When partners focus primarily on accountability,

the interaction can have a negative slant that permeates the group: "How did you mess up this week?"

5. Sometimes, out of the immaturity of group mem-
    bers, the process of confessing can become titillat-
    ing.

6. Focusing on accountability sets up participants to
    slip into what is known as "confessor's regret". The
    person,
who opens up and shares his struggles, doesn't come
    back because of regrets about sharing too much too
    fast in the relationship.

A Picture to Consider

One of the great events recorded in Scripture about the
earthly life of Jesus is the story of His
relationship with Martha, Mary and
their brother Lazarus (John 11:1-44).
The love that Jesus had for Martha,
Mary, and Lazarus is recorded at
least three times in the story. When
you read the account, you are drawn
into the feelings of the three family

> *God wants you
> to participate in
> the process of
> helping people
> grow and find
> freedom.*

members and how Jesus empathized with them; He felt
what they felt.

This familiar story tells us that Lazarus was sick and
his sisters sent for Jesus, but He did not come until after
Lazarus had been dead four days. The account covers
Martha's reaction to Jesus and follows with Mary's tearful
encounter with Jesus and His empathy with her and her
friends. "Jesus wept." (John 11:35). Then the most amazing thing happens. Jesus goes to the tomb and resurrects
Lazarus! He puts new life in that decaying, smelly body
and Lazarus floats out of the tomb.

At the conclusion of the story, there is a beautiful picture that shows what we pray A&E Partnerships and Groups will become. Jesus turns to Lazarus' friends, standing there in shocked disbelief, and tells them "Take off the grave clothes and let him go." Jesus involves the friends in taking those stinky grave clothes off Lazarus. The only one that could give life was and is Jesus but today, as then, He involves other people in the process of setting people free, removing the "grave clothes" that we struggle with.

God wants you to participate in the process of helping people grow and find freedom.

Opening Windows

The relationships that God wants you to develop with one another in the Church are relationships based on loving acceptance. God gave me the following image of how we are to relate to one another: a window through which a cool breeze can blow. We are to be open windows that God can use to touch another person's life.

> *Life and transformation come through the Holy Spirit.*

The quality of our relationships with our partners enables us to be a window into their lives through which the Holy Spirit can pass. Life and transformation come through the Spirit; He simply uses the relationship as an entry point.

When we are available to be instruments of God's unconditional love and acceptance and when we commit to the relationship, God can use us as His instruments to help remove our partner's "grave clothes". God's Spirit heals the wounds and gives new life; we are simply available to be His window, His instrument.

What Are A&E Partnerships and Groups?

An Accountability & Encouragement Partnership is

made up of three individuals who covenant together for deliberate face-to-face meetings "to encourage one another and build each other up" (I Thessalonians 5:11) toward a consistent walk in purity. A&E Partnerships have weekly meetings and sometimes daily check-ins with one another. Ideally, A&E Groups are made up of four A&E Partnerships that meet monthly for the mutual edification of one another. Each group has 12 people participating.

The A&E Partnership Covenant

A&E Partnerships are based on a covenant agreement that defines the intention and function of the partnership. The covenant has six agreements that serve as guidelines for the way the partnerships and groups work.

- AGREEMENT #1: AFFIRMATION
  This first agreement concerns unconditional love and acceptance (Romans 15:7).

  "With God's help, I will unconditionally love and accept you as my brother in Christ. There is nothing you have done or will do that will make me not accept you and love you as Christ has loved me. I may not agree or like what you do, but I will love you as a person Christ died for. I will do all I can do to hold you up in God's affirming love."

- AGREEMENT #2: AVAILABILITY
  This agreement concerns your availability to one another.

  "With God's help I will make available to you my time, energy, insight and material possessions. I am at your disposal if you have a need, to the limit of my resources and within the boundaries of my marriage and family covenants. I pledge you my time on a regular basis, whether in prayer or in an agreed-on meeting time."

- AGREEMENT #3: AUTHENTIC INTIMACY
This agreement involves the quality of the relationships with one another.

"With God's help, I will openly share the person I am with you by disclosing my feelings, my struggles, my joys and my hurts as God enables me to do so. I will seek to mirror back to you what I perceive you are saying or feeling, even if this involves risk and pain for both of us. By faith I will take that risk with you and 'speak the truth in love' (Ephesians 4:15). I will be sensitive to you and your feelings, your hurts and your wounds. With God helping me, I will be honest in a sensitive manner with you."

- AGREEMENT # 4: PRAYER
This agreement involves bringing one another before God on a regular basis.

"I covenant to pray for you daily, because I know that God wants His children to pray for one another and because God is the One who enables all of us to grow. I will ask God to give you wisdom, guidance, and blessings with a special emphasis on the issues that you are dealing with each day."

- AGREEMENT # 5: CONFIDENTIALITY
This agreement concerns the importance of confidentiality in the group.
"I covenant with you to keep whatever you share with me within the confines of the partnership and

I will trust you to do the same. This will enable us to be open and honest without fear of betrayal."

- AGREEMENT #6: ACCOUNTABILITY
  This agreement concerns the release and utilization of each other's gifts for the benefits of the other person.

  "I believe the gifts God has given me are for the common good and should be utilized for your benefit. When I discover areas of my life that are under bondage, hung up, or blocked by my own issues or the wounds and scars inflicted by others, I will seek Christ's liberating power through His Holy Spirit. I trust that He will use my covenant partners to help me see what He wants to heal and set free so I might be able to give more of myself to you. I am accountable to you to become what God has designed me to be."

(**Note:** These agreements are based on material from the book by Louie Evans, Jr. entitled Covenant To Care.)

What's Unique about A&E Partnerships?
There are several things that make A&E Partnerships different from many of the accountability groups or partnerships, counseling and growth groups, sponsorship relationships and other similar relationships within churches. Here are some of the unique aspects:

- The partnership is a three-way partnership, not a two way (Ecclesiastes 4:12). These partnership relationships participate once a month with a larger group for enrichment and fellowship. The larger group enables every one to keep a bigger picture of what God is accomplishing through His Church.

- Relationships are intentional, voluntary and mutual. Each person must freely agree to the covenants stated above and enter into the agreement with both partners.

- The partnerships are based on peer relationships of mutuality. The only authority is God. The submission of the partners, one to another (Ephesians 5:21), is what makes the partnerships work.

- Openness about feelings is one of the critical factors in the authentic relationships built in the partnerships (Romans 12:15). The "One Another Principles" given throughout the New Testament serve as directives for the relationships.

- Accountability is by submission, one to another, and not based on a top down check-up system. The Holy Spirit is the one responsible for the conviction of sin and repentance, not one of the Partners.

What Do You Do in A&E Partnerships?

The primary focus of A&E Partnerships is on the quality of relationship that is built between the partners. Bible study, prayer and fellowship, based on the early New Testament church model (Acts 2:42-47), are the primary ingredients the partnerships are built around. The covenant is critical since so many people in churches today do not know much about building authentic relationships.

Authentic relationships in the New Testament begin with the recognition of the importance of Christians connecting in love relationships. Jesus gave His great relational mandate when He said:

A new commandment I give you. Love one another. As I have loved you, os you must love one another. All men will know that you are my disciples if you love one another.

John 13:34-35

- We are commanded to love one another. This command is given sixteen times in the New Testament and it instructs us to initiate love relationships with one another.

- This is an awesome challenge for men in our culture. Too many men have never had loving relationships with another man, not even their fathers. Few things hinder men in their spiritual life like the absence of loving relationships.

- The "One Another Principles" given throughout the New Testament serve as directives and functional guidelines for the relationships.

- The next step in connecting with one another is service to one another. Jesus modeled this for the Disciples in John 13 and instructed us to do the same (John 13:1-17).

Paul's Model

Paul gives us a picture of how he worked with the men at Thessalonica.

We speak as men approved by God to be entrusted with the gospel. We are not trying to please men but God, who tests our hearts.

I Thessalonians 2:4

Paul said he had one audience and it was God who had approved of him. His accountability was to the Father.

As Apostles of Christ we could have been a burden to you, but we were gentle among you, like a mother caring for her little children.

I Thessalonians 2:7

He nurtured the men he worked with, with the tenderness of a mother nursing her infant.

We loved you so much that we were delighted to share with you not only the gospel of God, but our lives as well, because you had become so dear to us.

I Thessalonians 2:8

Paul shared his life with them. He modeled vulnerability and openness with his men.

You are witnesses and so is God, of how holy, righteous and blameless we were among you who believed.

I Thessalonians 2:10

He modeled for the men holy, righteous and blameless behaviors. He walked in purity before his men.

We dealt with each of you as a father deals with his own children, encouraging, comforting and urging you to live lives worthy of God, who calls you into his kingdom and glory.

I Thessalonians 2:11-12

Paul encouraged, comforted and urged his men to live lives worthy of God. He didn't focus on failures, endless confession, condemnation, shame and guilt.

If you function in your partnership as Paul did with his men in Thessalonica, your A&E Partnerships will function powerfully and your life and the lives of your partners will be transformed.

Outline of Partnership Meetings

The meetings between A&E Partners can take place in any setting that allows for freedom from interruptions and an atmosphere conducive to confidentiality while sharing. Public settings (restaurant, coffee shops, etc.) may not be conducive to confidentiality or prayer.

Suggested Guidelines for Meetings

- Each partner is responsible to be on time. Consistent tardiness can signal mixed motives and a lack of commitment.

- One of the partners opens with a brief prayer.

- Following the prayer, each partner logs in. "Logging in" is giving a brief report of victories for the week, the things that you see God doing in your life, followed by a brief statement about your desire to receive prayer for a specific issue.

- After each partner has logged in, all three discuss the Bible study homework they completed since the last meeting. (Bible Studies are provided in the A&E Partnership Manual.) The partners each share what God impressed on them through the study. The group reads through the passage and shares insights and applications. The focus is on building relationships in Christ and encouraging each one spiritually.

- Concerns, issues or slips from the week are discussed after the study time. (Guidelines for confessing "slips" are offered at the end of this chapter.) Specific encouragement and suggestions can be made during this time.

- After the open discussion time is completed, the group listens to each other's prayer requests. The meeting ends with prayer for each other. (See Guidelines for Conversational Prayer on the next page.)

- The length of meetings will vary depending on the needs and issues in each person's life. However, whenever possible, a suggested two hour time frame should be maintained.

- Conclude by setting the time for the next meeting. Meetings will be held weekly in the normal course of daily life, but may become more frequent when one or more of the partners is feeling a need for more time and interaction.

Guidelines for Conversational Prayer

Our purpose for prayer in small groups and A&E Partnerships is to have an experience of God's presence in the group relationship. We join our voices and our thoughts to lift our prayers to God in unity and to invite His Spirit to manifest Himself in our presence. On occasion, group prayer gets side tracked because one or more people feel led to sermonize to the group or to dominate the prayer time with long wordy prayers. In the New Testament there are no long wordy prayers recorded. Jesus and the

> *There are no long, wordy prayers recorded in the New Testament.*

apostles possibly prayed long prayers when they were off in the hills by themselves, but when they were together, the prayers were brief.

The key to effective group prayer is the heart attitude of those present. The Holy Spirit is always present when each participant seeks God's face with the other group members and the focus is on Jesus and the Father. When the focus is on Jesus, participants lose their desire to preach or teach other members in lengthy wordy prayers. Such group unity often opens the way for the Spirit to manifest Himself to us (Matthew 18:19-20).

Too often in small group prayer, each person will pray one time covering all the topics he wants to pray about. Some people sermonize in their prayers and other group members may tend to lose focus and concentration. Some have even been known to fall asleep!

Conversational prayer is quite different. Everyone, who wants to, prays but the prayer time is more inter-active and relational. In conversational prayer a series of topics is prayed for, one at a time, by all of the members. Each person can pray as many times as he wants to, but he keeps each prayer focused on the topic before the group. Prayers often are more spontaneous and the excitement of God's presence in each life can be felt.

For example a group may pray about the pending surgery for one of the group members. It might proceed like this:

Member # 1:   "Lord, I want to pray about Sam's surgery. I know he is nervous about it, Lord, so I pray you would comfort him."

Member # 2:   "I agree with that prayer, Lord. Please give Sam your peace."

Member # 3:   "And, Lord, I pray you would guide

	the surgeon's hands and let the surgery proceed without any problems or complications."
Member # 4:	"I agree with that prayer, Lord."
Member # 5	(Sam): "Thank you for these prayers, Lord, and I am so grateful that you have given me a group of friends for prayer and support."
(Pause/Silence)	
Member # 3:	"Lord, I want to pray also for the conference coming up this weekend."

Repeat the process, working through all the topics the group wants to pray about.

This style of prayer tends to focus group attention and energy on each topic and participants are less likely to find their minds wandering. Conversational prayer also helps the sermonizers change their ways of praying, creating more spiritual unity among participants.

> *The danger in teaching about prayer is that often people try to impose structures to be followed instead of allowing the Holy Spirit to lead.*

The danger in teaching about prayer is that people often try to impose structures to be followed instead of allowing the Spirit to lead. Conversational group prayer is intended to be free from structure and spontaneous. Do not let structure hinder your experience of group prayer. When people first begin to practice conversational prayer it doesn't feel spontaneous; it feels awkward. Practice together for a few weeks and see how it feels.

Guidelines to Facilitate
Conversational Prayer in a Small Group

- Each person in the group should have an understanding about conversational prayer (some instructions).

- Each participant should agree to keep prayers brief (5 or 6 sentences at the most).

- Each participant should pray about only one topic when he prays and should only change the topic if it is clear that everyone who wants to has prayed on the current topic.

- Participants may pray many times during a session of conversational prayer and brief prayers are appropriate. ("Thank you, Lord.") ("I agree.")

- After the group has covered the topics suggested for prayer, the leader will close.

- The group can agree to follow some simple guidelines about topics:

  - Begin with praise and thanksgiving.
  - Move to topics from outside the group.
  - Close with topics related to one another in the group.

Remember that prayer is talking with our Heavenly Father with the other group members participating as fellow family members. Group prayer works best when it is like a large loving family interacting around Daddy with every-one participating. The focus is on God the Father, Jesus and the Holy Spirit.

Daily Check-In Guidelines

When A&E Partners agree to check-in with each other on a daily basis, it is best if the telephone/email check-ins stay very positive.

- Share a victory, an encouraging word, a verse of Scripture.

- If the other person is having a rough day, pray for him and offer to check back in a few hours.

- Be real!

- Remember the emphasis is on encouraging one an-other, not in telling the other person how to fix their situation.

- If you share an idea that has helped you, always precede the comment with "Something that has re-ally helped me is..."
- Respect your A&E Partner's time and schedule.

- Save lengthy sharing for face-to-face meetings.

- End the check-in time with an expression of appre-ciation, gratitude or love.

A&E Group Guidelines

The monthly A&E Group meetings are designed to be less structured yet, at the same time, focused on encour-agement and relationship building. Meeting in someone's home is a good place to meet and refreshments are a good idea. The meeting can begin with prayer and worship but move quickly into sharing victories during the last month. Focus on what God is doing, not the struggles of the individuals. The idea is to help individuals stay focused on the positives, not on the painful.

> *Focus on what God is doing, not the struggles of the individuals.*

After sharing and rejoicing, ask for specific prayer requests. Divide the group into smaller groups (not their A&E Partners) and pray for one another. Conclude the meeting with announcements about the next meeting place and allow the people to fellowship afterwards.

Accountability Guidelines

In your A&E Partnerships, it is helpful to have a few guidelines for keeping your accountability on target. Some people feel they need to be confronted by their A&E Partners with what is known as accountability questions. That may be necessary in some instances, but the goal should be to build open spontaneous vulnerability with one another. Ideally, you should feel so closely connected to your two partners that you will regularly and freely make these confessions:

- I have not been with a woman (or any person) anywhere since we were last together that might be seen as compromising or "playing with fire" sexually.

- I have successfully utilized the CPR strategy and turned opportunities to lust into opportunities for prayer since we were last together.

- I have not exposed myself to any sexually explicit material since we were last together.

213

- I have spent adequate time in Bible study and prayer since we were last together.

- I have kept my mind free from sexual images and inappropriate fantasies.

- I have regularly prayed Psalm 139:23-24 and what God has been showing me about my woundedness since we were last together is…

- (If married) I have given priority time to my wife and family since we were last together.

- I would like your help with…

- I have not just lied to you in answering any of these questions.

In some situations using questions may be necessary if a person is sandbagging or has trouble honestly facing his issues.

Guidelines for Confessing "Slips"

Note: the term "slip" is somewhat innocuous and does not indicate the seriousness of the situation. The term "failure" sounds too final and discouraging. Since the word "encourage" means "to put the courage in", I made the decision to stick with the word "slip".

In an attempt to provide some protection and assistance for confessing slips in sexual accountability situations, these following items are suggested.

- The primary purpose of the A&E Partnership is to encourage one another to pursue purity through a closer walk with the Lord.

- A&E Partners do not need to know details of the slip. To assist in acknowledging the slip without the confession becoming titillating is always the goal.

- This classification system is suggested:

Level of Activity:
0—Normal sexual feelings (within God's design and boundaries)
1—Temptation (you put/allowed yourself to be in a tempting situation)
2—Lust (no acting out)
3—Pornography (no acting out.)
4—Acting out (with self)
5—Acting out (with others)

- It is appropriate to ask about the motivational emotional drivers that were at work in the person. "What were your emotional issues at the time you had the slip?"

- Ask if there were any unusual aspects to this slip.

- Ask the person how they recovered from the slip.

- Minister forgiveness to the person.

- Remember you are not in the group to listen to titillating details. Keep the focus on encouragement and edification.

The concerns that should be noted involve the following:
- Chronic slips in efforts to walk in purity: walking in purity should be similar to walking across a green grassy lawn. It should go smoothly, but occasionally

you might step in a pile of dog poop. When a person is chronically stepping in the piles, then further assistance may be needed such as a Twelve Step Group, counseling, or treatment.

• Consistent anger issues: when anger issues consistently show up in slips the anger has to be addressed.

• Consistent failure to keep the A&E Covenant: when the individual chronically fails to maintain the A&E Partnership covenant, it is appropriate to suggest he examine his commitment to the process.

Some people are not able or ready to be part of an A&E Partnership. Referral to counseling, treatment or a Twelve Step Group may be the best alternative for some individuals.

CHAIN BREAKERS

√ You cannot win the battle alone. God has designed the whole process to draw you into relationships with other people.

√ Encouragement is what you need, people who will put courage into you.

√ Covenants are never to be taken lightly. You benefit from a covenant relationship to the degree you invest in that relationship.

√ Having A&E partners is not like being sent to the Principal's office. An A&E Partner is like a coach w ho cares about you and wants you to win.

√ Prayer is talking to God. Conversational prayer is a group conversation with God.

√ You can walk in purity by the power of the Holy Spirit and the assistance of a couple of friends.

Section Five

Passion for Purity

Chapter Fifteen

"Winning the Battle Spiritually"

Winning the battle over sexual immorality and temptation begins with the heart, soul and spirit of a man (an inside job!). Jesus said that sexual immorality is from the heart (Matthew 15:19; Mark 7:21-23). Paul said it is from the sinful nature in man (Galatians 5:19). Winning the battle involves changing you on the inside, changing your heart attitudes. You need a new heart, a new inner person to win the battle.

You will find it helpful to read this next section with your Bible. You may want to mark the verses so you will be able to find them again in the future.

A New Heart

God spoke through the prophet Ezekiel:

I will cleanse you from all your impurities and from all your idols. I will give you a new heart and put a new spirit in you; I will remove from you your heart of stone and give you a heart of flesh. And I will put my spirit in you and move you to follow my decrees and be careful to keep my laws.

Ezekiel 36:25-27

God's promise to His people is that He will change their hearts and put a new spirit in them that will enable them to live by His purposes ("follow my decrees") and to carefully keep His laws. Christianity is about changing your heart and character, then providing you with the ability to live righteously by God's power. The Holy Spirit enables you to win the battle and to live a victorious life.

> *Christianity is the only world religion that speaks of a God who changes your heart and character.*

Christianity is the only world religion that speaks of a God who changes your heart and character. The religions of the world look to man's efforts for self-discipline and perseverance to change his own behavior and character. A person has to engage in some ritual, meditation, study or suffering prescribed by his religion. He believes that, through his own efforts, he will in time become more moral or righteous by the standards of his god. Christianity is about God invading your life and enabling you to live, by His power, life on a different moral plane.

No Wonder You Can't!

> Just because you go to church and hang out with Christians doesn't mean that your life has been transformed by God.

Some of you are trying to live a moral life with an old heart. No wonder you are not able to win the battle over sexual immorality. Just because you go to church and hang out with Christians does not mean that your life has been transformed by God. You may have never come to the realization of God's provision and power. Some of you may think of yourselves as Christians because you were born in America or because you go to church. Being a Christian is not about what you do. It is about what Christ has done!

There are many nice people who appear to be moral, but who are not Christians. The only way to have your heart changed is through Jesus Christ. If your heart has not been changed by your Christian experience, please read the rest of this chapter carefully. You cannot win the battle spiritually in your own strength.

The Old Nature

Scripture teaches that all people have sinned and do

not live up to God's standards,

For all have sinned and fall short of the glory of God.
Romans 3:23

and because of this, everyone deserves punishment for his/her sinfulness.

For the wages of sin is death, but the gift of God is eternal life in Christ Jesus our Lord.
Romans 6:23

Men's hearts are deceitful,

The heart is deceitful above all things and beyond cure. Who can understand it?
Jeremiah 17:9

and the motives of their hearts are what God monitors. Your basic old nature is that of a sinner.

There is nothing concealed that will not be disclosed, or hidden that will not be made known. What you have said in the dark will be heard in the daylight, and what you have whispered in the ear in the inner rooms will be proclaimed from the roofs.
Luke 12:2-3

Often individuals think, "If it doesn't hurt anyone, it can't be a sin." or "If she is willing to participate with me in having sex, then it can't be a sin." God says your heart attitude of lusting for another person is the same as adultery. There are few men who can pass a "heart test" on the lust issue.

But I tell you that anyone who looks at a woman lustfully has already committed adultery with her in his heart.
Matthew 5:28

Before God, you are a sinner and your decision to turn

from your sinful attitudes is the beginning point for you to receive a new heart. This turning from sin to God is called repentance. It is the necessary first step to win the battle spiritually.

What Did Jesus Die For?

The Bible says that Jesus died for you! You are a sinner (as are all humans) and if you had to pay the penalty for your own sin, you would have to die spiritually and be separated from God for all eternity (Romans 6:23).

The Bible says that Jesus died for all!

Every person is a living soul. As said before, each person is a "soul with skin on". The human body is the container of the real you and the real you, your soul, will live forever, either with God for eternity or separate from God for eternity.

The person you have lusted after or engaged in sexual activities with is a "soul with skin on", too. And that person will live for eternity either with God or separate from God. Get the picture? Since the wages of sin is death, then individuals, who die without ever coming to Christ, have to pay the penalty for their sin . . . eternal separation from God. You have to pay the penalty and your sexual partner has to pay the penalty unless . . .

Unless...

...someone else pays the penalty for your sins. This is what Jesus did. This is the reason Jesus had to die. He came into the world to pay for every man's sin. Jesus' death on the cross was God's judgment on the sin of man.

But God demonstrates his own love for us in this: While we were still sinners, Christ died for us.

Romans 5:8

222

He is the atoning sacrifice for our sins, and not only for ours but also for the sins of the whole world.

1 John 2:2

This is how we know what love is: Jesus Christ laid down his life for us.

1 John 3:16

Jesus came to die for man's sin so that every person who puts his faith in Jesus will be justified and reconciled to God.

Since we have now been justified by his blood, how much more shall we be saved from God's wrath through him! For if, when we were God's enemies, we were reconciled to him through the death of his Son, how much more, having been reconciled, shall we be saved through his life!

Romans 5:9-10

You can be justified and reconciled to God. So can each of the sexual partners you have ever been with. When anyone accepts the death of Jesus as the payment for his sins, he will be justified.

Paul says that Jesus took your sins and gave you His life and His righteousness.

God made him (Jesus) who had no sin to be sin for us, so that in him we might become the righteousness of God.

2 Corinthians 5:17

When you put your faith in the sacrificial death of Jesus you become a new creation and you are delivered from the power of sin.

If anyone is in Christ, he is a new creation; the old has gone, the new has come!

2 Corinthians 5:17

Now you have a choice about the way you choose to live.

I put this in human terms because you are weak in your natural selves. Just as you used to offer the parts of your body in slavery to impurity and to ever-increasing wickedness, so now offer them in slavery to righteousness leading to holiness. When you were slaves to sin, you were free from the control of righteousness. What benefit did you reap at that time from the things you are now ashamed of? Those things result in death! But now that you have been set free from sin and have become slaves to God, the benefit you reap to holiness, and the result is eternal life.

Romans 6:19-22

When you accept Jesus Christ's death for your sins you have peace with God. This new life and peace are the gifts of God by His grace.

For it is by grace you have been saved, through faith…and this is not from yourselves, it is the gift of God…not by works, so that no one can boast.

Ephesians 2:8-9

To become a true Christian, to be born again, to receive a new heart, you must accept Jesus' sacrificial death as payment for your sins. When you do, you will receive forgiveness from all your sins…

If we walk in the light, as He is in the light, we have fellowship with one another, and the blood of Jesus, His son, purifies us from all sin.

1 John 1:7

If we confess our sins, He is faithful and just and will forgive us our sins and purify us from all unrighteousness.

1 John 1:9

…and a freedom and power to live a life that is pleasing to God.

Those who live according to the sinful nature have their minds set on what that nature desires; but those who live in accordance with the Spirit have their minds set on what the Spirit desires. The mind of sinful man is death, but the mind controlled by the Spirit is life and peace; the sinful nature is hostile to God. It does not submit to God's law, nor can it do so. Those controlled by the sinful nature cannot please God.

Romans 8:5-8

Step of Faith

If there is any doubt in your mind about whether your life has been transformed by Christ, then it would be a great idea to make sure. Unless you are right with God on this issue, you will never win the battle.

To make sure, pray and ask God to help. Pray a prayer to God (talk with Him as you would a good friend sitting in the room with you) and tell Him your heart's desire is to be changed. Thank Him for allowing Jesus to die for your sins and tell God that you accept Jesus' death as the payment for your sins. Invite God to come into your life and bring you His peace and His freedom.

Step of Faith Prayer

Father God, I desire to have you change my life. Thank you for sending Jesus to die for my sins and to set me free so I can change and grow. I accept what Jesus did at the Cross as payment for my sins. Come into my life, take charge of my life and heal my wounds. Make me the person you want me to be.

Bring me your freedom and peace. Amen.

The New Life

If you prayed the above prayer as suggested, then you have started a new life with God. It is what most Christians call being "born again." When you accept Jesus' death on the Cross and allow God to take control of your life, you become a new creation (II Corinthians 5:17). You might not feel any different at this moment, but be assured if you sincerely prayed and asked God to forgive you and give you a new life, He did just that!

If you have an A&E Partnership, it would be great for you to share with them that you prayed and invited Christ into your life. They will rejoice with you and can assist you in this new life. Ask them to pray for you as you grow.

What About...

Some of you may be thinking, "But I have been a Christian for years and I still struggle! Why can't I win the battle spiritually?"

You are the reason this book has been written. I want to help you win the battle. My prayer is that you will gain a better understanding of the "why" of your struggle from reading these pages. Each individual Christian's struggle is unique in terms of the emotional needs and wounds that amplify his/her sexual impulses. But the solution is the same for each person. We look at how we walk in purity in Chapter Sixteen.

CHAIN BREAKERS

√ Christianity is not something you do. Christianity is about God changing your heart and character.

√ Going to church does not make you a Christian anymore than going to a hamburger stand makes you a cheeseburger!

√ Repentance, turning from sin, is the necessary first step toward a changed life.

√ Jesus died for you. If you had been the only sinner in the world, He would have died just for you.

√ God is more concerned about your spiritual life than you are because He loves you and has staked His glory on you. (Isaiah 48:10-11)

Chapter Sixteen
"Walking in Purity"

It is God's will that you should be holy; that you should avoid sexual immorality; that each of you should learn to control his own body in a way that is holy and honorable, not in passionate lust like the heathen, who do not know God; and that in this matter no one should wrong his brother or take advantage of him. The Lord will punish men for all such sins, as we have already told you and warned you. For God did not call us to be impure but to live a holy life. Therefore, he who rejects this instruction does not reject man but God, who gives you his Holy Spirit.

1 Thessalonians 4:3-8

There are several points to pull from this passage:

- It is God's will that you should be holy.

- You should avoid sexual immorality.

- You should learn to control your own body in a way that is holy and honorable.

- You should not give your body over to passionate lust.

- You should not wrong your brother/sister or take advantage of him/her in sexual matters.

- The Lord will punish men for all such sins.

- God did not call you to be impure, but to live a holy life.

- If you reject these instructions, you are rejecting God, not man.

Jesus never promised that lust would cease being an issue in the life of a Christian. Paul is not saying that either. Scriptures teach that the same faith that brings you salvation is also the faith that enables you to live a pure life. The fact you are struggling against temptations of the flesh is confirmation that the Spirit of God lives in you. Faith that justifies is the faith that perseveres in the fight against lust.

> A dog in the hunt doesn't stop to scratch fleas.

As John Piper writes in his book, *Future Grace*: "We fight to be so satisfied with all that God is for us in Jesus that the temptation to sin loses its power over us."

An old country boy preacher says, *"A dog in the hunt doesn't stop to scratch fleas."* A focus on a higher purpose overrides the temptation to be distracted by other issues. Yet some people continue to struggle as Christians because they don't have a battle plan offering freedom from these other issues.

Battle Plan

We as Christian men, who have struggled in battle, know we must continue fighting. Here is the battle plan we follow:

1. Admit that you cannot win the battle without God's intervention.

2. Repent and confess your failure to God.

3. Pray and ask God to show you the issues that amplify your sexual impulses.

4. Establish one or more relationships to encourage you and hold you accountable to continue to grow spiritually.

5. Present the issues to God, one by one, and ask Him to heal them and enable you to find healthier ways of meeting your emotional needs.

6. Intentionally submit yourself to God's transformational healing process.

7. Persevere!

Winning in the Trenches

"Nothing worth having comes without some kind of fight. You have to kick at the darkness until it bleeds daylight."
Musician Bruce Cockburn

There is a battle going on all the time in the heart of every true Christian. It is the battle between the cravings of our selfish human fleshly desires and the desires of the forces of God at work in us.

So I say, live by the Spirit, and you will not gratify the desires of your sinful nature. For the sinful nature desires what is contrary to the Spirit, and the Spirit what is contrary to the sinful nature. They are in conflict with each other, so that you do not do what you want.
Galatians 5:16-17

The picture Paul presents here is a picture of a permanent attitude of opposition. Biblically, the flesh is always warring against the Spirit. Commentator Kenneth S. Wuest uses the image of trench warfare to describe the conflict. Two opposing forces establish their positions and dig a series of trenches for the purpose of holding the territory. Each force has entrenched itself for a long drawn-out battle.

Spiritual Warfare

The Christian life must be understood as warfare. Many Christians approach the Christian life like it is a Sunday School picnic, when it is really more like a landing on Normandy Beach.

We expect a picnic, but suddenly we realize that people, all around us, are getting shot and blown to pieces. We have spread a picnic blanket on the sandy battlefield of war.

When you fight a war, you take casualties. The Christian life is not safe. It was not meant to be. Wars are won on the offensive, not the defensive.

> **Wars are won on the offensive, not the defensive!**

Paul describes his personal conflict in the seventh chapter of Romans and concludes with the agonizing plea (I have paraphrased), "Who will rescue me from the battle?" (verse 24). He answers his own plea with: "Thanks be to God – through Jesus Christ our Lord!" (verse 25).

Paul gives his instruction to Christians about how to live in the middle of this trench warfare:

> *Let us behave decently, as in the daytime, not in orgies and drunkenness, not in sexual immorality and debauchery, not in dissension and jealousy. Rather clothe yourselves with the Lord Jesus Christ, and do not think about how to gratify the desires of your sinful nature.*
>
> Romans 13:13-14

In the original language "do not think about how to gratify the desires" literally means: "make no provision for." When you are living in the realm of the Spirit, you make no provision for the cravings of the flesh. Living in the realm of the Spirit means to wear the Spirit's power like you wear a suit of clothes. In our society we like to say "the clothes make the man," even though we know that bad character cannot be hidden for long behind nice clothes. But in the Spiritual realm the "clothes" you wear produce Christian character, the fruit of the Spirit.

> We fight the battle in the trenches. We win because we know the promises of God are greater than the promises of sin.

We fight the battle in the trenches and we win because we know the promises of God are greater than the promises of sin. We are enabled to battle and win by the indwelling power of the Holy Spirit.

Setting the Heart Free!

Sensuality is an attachment of the heart, and our hearts must be set free. Those who are enslaved by this attachment have searched for ways to find freedom. Christians have tried three strategies to address this epidemic of sensuality in our culture. Only one of the strategies produces lasing victory in the battle.

- Education Strategy: In this strategy the belief is that if a person has enough education, that person will make healthy appropriate choices. It is true that people will likely make different choices with education, but that does not imply they will have character. The optimistic belief is that people can be educated into character and healthier choices. While education is part of the solution, there is ample evidence that <u>education does not change the basic character of people.</u> There is no significant correlation between more education and better character. An appropriate example is in the issue of obesity. While education has helped change some community attitudes about obesity, there are well-educated people still choosing to overeat. The same is true about smoking and sexual issues. More education, even Christian education, about sexuality has not fostered better decisions. Character is not built just with education, and purity will not be maintained just with education.

• Self-control Strategy: Christians are challenged and encouraged to maintain better self-control. It is reinforced by accountability structures and external consequences so individuals won't make wrong choices. Since this appeal does not address heart motives and emotional issues, it will breakdown under stress and in secrecy. White-knuckled self-control does not win battles against immorality over the long haul.

Most people I know wish the Christian life were this simple: "I know what I should do, so I do it." But the reality is that we all know more about how we should live than actually living that way.

• Spiritual Strategy: The numerous expressions of the hugely successful Twelve Step Program have validated the importance of the intervention of God to help people change their hearts and affections. Change happens and character is built as a person intentionally submits himself to God's transforming process. This is not about religion. It is about internal transformation by the power of God.

Only God can set the heart free from its attachments. When you give yourself over to sexual sensuality, even once, it changes the way you view life. You will forever see things with a sexual slant. Unless and until God heals your perspective, your heart will stay distracted by the promises of sexual sin and attached to the pleasure.

The only way to displace the human heart from its attachment to and love for sensual pleasure is to set forth a more worthy strategy. Only a powerful challenging strategy that demands a grand commitment, a big "yes", will ever displace the heart's affections.

An athlete, pursuing an Olympic gold medal, forsakes many of life's pleasures for a chance to win the medal. The desire and the challenge to go for the gold medal enables the athlete to detach from his heart's attachment to less worthy strategies.

> *There is only one option powerful enough and big enough to free the human heart from lustful attachments.*

There is only one strategy powerful enough and big enough to free the human heart from lustful attachments. It is the promise that comes when a life connects with God and finds satisfaction in what He promises. God is the only one who can set my heart and your heart free from all our sinful, unhealthy attachments. He is the source of all purity.

Maintaining Purity

In the Gospel of John we have a picture of what purity means through the interaction of Jesus with Peter (about washing his feet):

He [Jesus] came to Simon Peter, who said to him, 'Lord, are you going to wash my feet?' Jesus replied, 'You do not realize now what I am doing, but later you will understand.'

'No,' said Peter, 'you will never wash my feet.' Je-sus answered, 'Unless I wash you, you have no part with me.'

'Then, Lord,' Simon Peter replied, 'not just my feet but my hands and my head as well!'

Jesus answered, 'A person who has had a bath needs only to wash his feet; his whole body is clean. And you are clean...'

John 13:6-10

Jesus is saying since you have been justified (bathed), you need only cleanse that part of you that has become soiled by the world. Washing of the feet in this incident appears to teach the importance of cleansing ourselves from the things in the world that pollute or contaminate our lives. This is the internal purging that occurs when we confess our sins to God.

Learning through Consequences

Anyone can do sex. It takes maturity to walk in purity. It is easy to go with our sensual feelings, but it's hard to live with the consequences of taking the easy path. It takes maturity to live and walk in purity, and the consequences are much more enjoyable.

Remember David, the great Hebrew King we referred to earlier. We can learn a lot about walking in purity from David and we can also learn about the consequences of taking the easy path. Chuck Swindoll, in his excellent book on David's life, wrote:

"The only one in all of Scripture to be called 'a man after God's own heart', this single individual is mentioned more than any other Old Testament character in the pages of the New Testament. Poet, musician, courageous warrior and national statesman, David distinguished himself as one of God's greatest men . . . But he was anything but perfect. Having earned the public's trust and respect, he forfeits it all in a brief season of sensual pleasure."
Charles Swindoll, *David*

The story of David's life strikes all of us, touching some more painfully than others. God provided amazing details of David's sins so we each can have a vivid picture of where immorality leads and the bitter harvest that follows.

(**Note:** David's life has many more things to teach us than

236

we can focus on here. I highly recommend Swindoll's great biography David: A Man of Passion and Destiny for an in-depth look at this great man of God.)

Another writer makes a point from David's life about sowing and reaping:

"When David sowed to the flesh, he reaped what the flesh produced. Moreover, he reaped the consequences of his actions even though he had confessed his sin and had been forgiven for it. Underline it, star it, mark it deeply upon your conscious mind: Confession and forgiveness in no way stop the harvest. He had sown; he was to reap. Forgiven he was, but the consequences continued. This is exactly the emphasis Paul is giving the Galatians (Galatians 6:7-8) even in this age of grace. We are not to be deceived, for God will not be mocked. What we sow we will reap, and there are no exceptions."

John W. Lawrence, *Life Choices*

David's story is the account of a great man who had a great fall and faced great consequences from his sin with Bathsheba. Yet, he is remembered as a "man after God's own heart" and he was used by God to write some of the most beautiful words ever penned by man.

Praise the Lord, O my soul;
all my inmost being, praise his holy name.
Praise the Lord, O my soul, and forget not all his benefits –
who forgives all your sins and heals all your diseases,
who redeems your life from the pit
and crowns you with love and compassion,
who satisfies your desires with good things
so that your youth is renewed like the eagle's.

Psalm 103:1-5

The Lord is compassionate and gracious,
slow to anger abounding in love.
He will not always accuse,
nor will he harbor his anger forever;
He does not treat us as our sins deserve
or repay us according to our iniquities.
For as high as the heavens are above the earth,
so great is his love for those who fear him;
As far as the east is from the west,
so far as he removed our transgressions from us.
Psalm 103:8-12

King David was in his fifties when he fell into sin. God restored him; David was recycled by God's grace and mercy. He was allowed to keep his throne, but violence and rebellion from his own son broke his heart. Swindoll writes about David's grief when he learns of his son Absalom's death (II Samuel 18:33).

"David is a beaten man. He's strung out, sobbing as if he's lost his mind. Every crutch is removed. He's at the bitter end, broken and bruised, twisted and confused. The harvesting of his sins is almost more than he can bear."
Charles Swindoll, *David*

God does forgive. God does restore the years the locusts have eaten (Joel 2:25), and He does use all of our consequences to teach and train us. We learn from the consequences of our sins just as David did. This is true of sexual immorality and it is true of all our other sins.

Allow God to Guide You into Purity

It is important that you allow God to guide you into purity. The Holy Spirit will bring conviction to you and a sense of Godly sorrow concerning the things He wants to

remove from your life. When
you commit yourself to remove these pollutants and ask
Him for help, He will enable you to "put away" the things
He wants put away.

> *If we walk in the light as He is in the light, we have fellowship with one another and the blood of Jesus, His Son, purifies us from all sin.*
>
> 1 John 1:7

The Holy Spirit does this in two ways:

1) He convicts the person and makes him aware of the sin in his life, enabling him to put the sin out of his life.

2) He produces Christ-like character traits called "fruit of the Spirit" in the person's life.

When a person is living in the realm of the Spirit he is allowing the Spirit to have control over his life to accomplish these two tasks.

The relationship God expects us to have with Him is an impossible one unless His Spirit has done a supernatural work in us. What God desires is not just good behavior. He wants you and me to function from a totally new disposition whereby we can live a totally new life.

The Christian character we are to express in our daily lives is not "good doing", but "God-likeness". When the Spirit of God transforms you and me on the inside, we will exhibit Divine character traits and qualities ("Fruit of the Spirit"), not just reformed good human qualities. Oswald Chambers says, *"The characteristic of a disciple is not that he does good things, but that he is good in motive, because he has been made good by the supernatural grace of God."*

239

How Do We Walk in Purity?

We get to choose each moment to walk in purity or to walk in sin. All sins that you and I can commit are future sins. Sins from our past are gone! The only way we can sin is in the future, the next moment.

When we talk about walking in purity, we are talking about being free from sins of immorality in the future. When we speak of walking or living by faith, we are talking about faith we will exercise in the future.

The question each moment is which will you choose: sin or faith? Paul says (Romans 14:23) that we can't choose both. Can God be trusted to meet your needs in this next moment or will you look to your own resources to satisfy your needs? Satan holds out an attractive option. He whispers in your ear that his option will be better than trusting God and His promises. Satan's only hope is that he can blind you to the beauty of Christ by the promise of immediate gratification and get you to choose sin in this next moment.

> *Can God be trusted to meet your needs in this next moment or will you look to your own resources to satisfy your needs?*

What this means is that walking in purity is a lifelong battle fought each moment of every day. It is specifically a battle against sin and a battle for faith. Will you trust the promised gratification that comes through sin or will you trust the promised satisfaction that comes through faith? The choice is yours to make.

John Piper expresses the battle like this:

"Some sexual image comes into my mind and beckons me to pursue it. The way this temptation gets its power is by persuading me to believe that I will be happier if I follow it. The power of all temptation is the prospect that it will make me happier. No one

240

sins out of a sense of duty, when what they really want is to do what's right."

John Piper, Future Grace

He then adds:

"Our chief enemy is the lie that says sin will make our future happier. Our chief weapon is the Truth that says God will make our future happier. And faith is the victory that overcomes the lie, because faith is satisfied with God."

"The fight against lust is the fight to stay satisfied with God."

John Piper, Future Grace

Motivation

As you mature in your faith, God heals your wounds and transforms your character. Purity becomes the norm for your daily walk. Occasional skirmishes may occur, but your confidence is in God. His promises will enable you to soar with the eagle and not worry about how to cross the rivers and canyons that used to distract you.

Again I quote John Piper:

"We fight to be so satisfied with all that God is for us in Jesus that the temptation to sin loses its power over us."

John Piper, Future Grace

Our motivation for purity is our love for God and our desire to be pleasing to Him. This is what we fight for and why we battle to win.

When we choose to let God work in us and through us, we win the battle. We desire to be pleasing to the Father, to hear His affirmation, "Well done, my good and faithful servant" (Matthew 25:21,23).

The challenge for all of us is to live lives that are pleasing to God the Father and to live this kind of life in the power of His Spirit. It takes maturity to walk in purity. It is a walk worthy of your highest commitment and most diligent effort. It is a heroic endeavor!

CHAIN BREAKERS

√ Focus on a higher purpose and other issues will not be a distraction.

√ Make no provision for the cravings of the flesh.

√ Intentionally submit yourself to God's transforming process. Only God can set your heart free from lustful attachments.

√ Repentance and confession bring God's forgiveness and spiritual restoration, but the consequences of your actions may go on for years. Please remember that you reap what you sow.

√ God's promises can be trusted more than the promises of immorality. Learn and remember that a heart satisfied in God and His Word sets you free for future joy.

√ Your love for Jesus will defeat temptation and break the chains of your sin.

Epilogue

All heroic endeavors are difficult. The Christian life is a heroic endeavor and it is gloriously difficult.

It takes no heroic effort and few brains to live a life of sensual indulgence. Anyone can yield to sexual urges . . . but it takes a heroic effort to work out your salvation (Philippians 2:12-13) in practical living. We have to intentionally choose to not let sensual urges dominate our lives.

If we intentionally choose to obey the Spirit of God and practice in our physical life what God has put in us by His Spirit, then when the temptations come, we will find that our own nature, as well as the grace of God, will enable us to do the difficult, but right thing.

"It is always necessary to make an effort to be noble. Our salvation is a wonderful glorious thing, but it is also a heroic, holy thing. It tests us for all we are worth. Jesus is bringing many sons into glory and God will not shield you and me from the requirements of a son. God's grace turns out men and women with a strong family likeness to Jesus Christ..."
Oswald Chambers, *My Utmost for His Highest*

It takes a tremendous amount of discipline to live the noble life of a disciple of Jesus in a sensual, sex-saturated society. But with intentional effort and the enabling power of the Holy Spirit, you and I can accomplish this noble, heroic goal . . . to become like Jesus Christ and to be light and salt to dying people in a dying world.

Subject Index

Bibliography

Oswald Chambers, *My Utmost for His Highest* (Westwood, New Jersey: Barbour and Company, Inc., 1935)

J.D. Douglas, Editor, *The New Bible Dictionary* (Grand Rapids, Michigan: Wm. B. Eerdmans Publishing Company).

John Eldredge, *Wild at Heart* (Nashville, Tennessee: Thomas Nelson, Inc., 2001).

Louis H. Evans, Jr., *Covenant to Care* (Wheaton, Illinois: Victor Books, 1982).

Dr. Craig Glickman, *Solomon's Song of Love* (West Monroe, Louisiana: Howard Publishing, 2004).

Rom Harre, Roger Lamb, *The Encyclopedic Dictionary of Psychology* (Cambridge, Massachusetts: The MIT Press, 1983).

Shad Helmstetter, *The Self-Talk Solution* (New York, New York: William Morrow & Company, Inc., 1987).

Roberta Hestenes, *Using the Bible in Groups* (Philadelphia, Pennsylvania: The Westminster Press, 1983).

John W. Lawrence, *Life's Choices* (Portland, Oregon: Multnomah Press, 1975).

C.S. Lewis, *The Four Loves* (Glasgow: Fontana Books, 1960).

Harold Lindsell, Editor, *The Best of C. S. Lewis* (New York, New York: The Iverson Associates, 1969).

Leanne Payne, *Crisis in Masculinity* (Westchester, Illinois: Crossway Books, 1985).

Leanne Payne, *Restoring the Christian Soul* (Grand Rapids,

Michigan: Baker Books, 1991).

Tim Stafford, *The Sexual Christian* (Wheaton, Illinois: Victor Books, 1989).

Charles Swindoll, *David, A Man of Passion & Destiny* (Dallas, Texas: Word Publishing, 1997).

Merrill F. Unger, *Unger's Bible Dictionary* (Chicago. Illinois: Moody Press, 1957).

Denis Waitley, *Seeds of Greatness* (Old Tappan, New Jersey: Fleming H. Revell Company, 1983).

Maurice E. Wagner, *The Sensation of Being Somebody* (Grand Rapids, Michigan: Zondervan Publishing House, 1975).

Douglas Weiss, *Sex, Men and God* (Lake Mary, Florida: Siloam Press, 2002).

John White, *Eros Defiled* (Downers Grove, Illinois: Inter Varsity Press, 1977).

John White, *Eros Redeemed* (Downers Grove, Illinois: Inter Varsity Press, 1993).

Kenneth S. Wuest, *Golden Nuggets from the Greek New Testament* (Grand Rapids, Michigan: Wm. B. Eerdmans Publishing Company, 1940).

Recommended Reading List

Neil T. Anderson, *The Bondage Breaker*

Neil T. Anderson, *Victory over the Darkness*

Stephen Arteburn, Fred Stoeker, Mile Yorkey, *Everyman's Battle*

Mike Cleveland, *Pure Freedom*

John Eldredge, *Waking the Dead*

Chip Ingram, *Love, Sex, and Lasting Relationships*

Brennan Manning, *Abba's Child*

Tommy Nelson, *The Book of Romance*

David A. Seamands, *Healing for Damaged Emotions*

David A. Seamands, *Redeeming the Past*

Maurice E. Wagner, *Anger's Fire Extinguisher*

Sandra D. Wilson, *Into Abba's Arms*

Sandra D. Wilson, *Released from Shame*

Dr. Waylon O. Ward
is the Executive Director of Mercy Matters
and Global Fathering Initiative.

P.O. Box 275
Colleyville, TX 76034

214-415-3486

waylon@mercymatters.com
www.globalfathering.com